THE DESIGNER'S GUIDE TO
MARKETING AND PRICING

THE DESIGNER'S GUIDE TO
MARKETING
AND PRICING

how to win clients and what to charge them

Ilise Benun and Peleg Top
founders of Marketing-Mentor.com

BOOKS
Cincinnati, Ohio
www.howdesign.com

For more fine books from F+W Publications, visit www.fwpublications.com.

12 11 10   5 4 3

Distributed in Canada by Fraser Direct, 100 Armstrong Avenue, Georgetown, Ontario, Canada L7G 5S4, Tel: (905) 877-4411. Distributed in the U.K. and Europe by David & Charles, Brunel House, Newton Abbot, Devon, TQ12 4PU, England, Tel: (+44) 1626 323200, Fax: (+44) 1626 323319, E-mail: postmaster@davidandcharles.co.uk. Distributed in Australia by Capricorn Link, P.O. Box 704, Windsor, NSW 2756 Australia, Tel: (02) 4577-3555.

Library of Congress Cataloging-in-Publication Data

Benun, Ilise, 1961-
 The designer's guide to marketing and pricing : how to win clients and what to charge them / Ilise Benun and Peleg Top. -- 1st ed.
     p. cm.
 Includes bibliographical references and index.
 ISBN 978-1-60061-008-0 (pbk. : alk. paper)
 1. Marketing. 2. Pricing. I. Top, Peleg. II. Title.
 HF5415.B42944 2008
 658.8--dc22   2007051923

Edited by Amy Schell
Designed by Grace Ring
Production coordinated by Greg Nock

ACKNOWLEDGMENTS

The material in this book springs from many different sources: from our own experiences over the last twenty years and from those of our clients, our colleagues and even the people in our personal relationship circles. But without the designers we have known, we would not have been able to write this book, much less develop the material. So we begin by thanking everyone we've ever worked with for allowing us to observe and learn from their experiences.

We are especially grateful to the great folks at F+W Publications, who have supported this work from its inception, by giving both of us our first speaking gigs, and Ilise her very first published article and then, ten years later, her first published book (*Self Promotion Online*, 2001). Without *HOW* Magazine, HOW Books and the HOW Design Conference, we would not be where we are today. That is a fact.

We'd like to specifically thank Amy Schell, who approached us after we gave the Pricing and Marketing Workshop at the HOW Design Conference in 2006 and said, "This needs to be a book." From there, she smoothly shepherded us through the process. We also thank Amy for being the most flexible editor a pair of writers could have. She knows when to step in and when to step out of the process. Also, we are grateful to all F+W staff we've encountered over the years, in particular Bryn Mooth, Sara Dumford and Colleen Cannon. And to David Baker, Emily Cohen and Robert Middleton for allowing us to reprint their material—because we could not have said it better.

ABOUT THE AUTHORS

 **Ilise Benun** is the co-founder of Marketing Mentor, as well as an author and national speaker.

Her books include *Stop Pushing Me Around: A Workplace Guide for the Timid, Shy and Less Assertive* (Career Press, June 2006), *Self-Promotion Online* and *Designing Web Sites:// for Every Audience* (HOW Design Books). She is also co-author of *The Art of Self Promotion* and *PR for Dummies, 2ⁿᵈ Edition*. She has been featured in *The New York Times, Inc. Magazine, Self, Essence, Crain's New York Business, HOW* Magazine and *Working Woman*. She has given presentations for national and international trade organizations, including The HOW Design Conference, American Marketing Association, Business Marketing Association, AIGA, Graphic Artists Guild, Registered Graphic Designers of Ontario and NY Designs—a program of LaGuardia Community College/CUNY.

Benun started her Hoboken, NJ-based consulting firm in 1988 and has been self-employed for all but three years of her working life. She has a BA in Spanish from Tufts University.

 **Peleg Top** is an entrepreneur, a business coach, a consultant and a mentor to the creative industry. After more than sixteen years running Top Design (www.topdesign.com), a successful *and* profitable Los Angeles-based design firm, he now focuses on helping designers market and brand themselves while becoming smarter and happier business owners. Top has spoken at industry conferences, including the HOW Design Conference and has also authored design books including *Design for Special Events: 500 of the Best Logos, Invitations and Graphics* (Rockport 2008) and *Letterhead and Logo Design 8* (Rockport 2003).

In 2003, he and Ilise Benun co-founded Marketing-Mentor (www.marketing-mentor.com), a one-on-one mentoring program and marketing resource center for the creatively self-employed.

Peleg currently resides in Silverlake, California with his partner of eleven years and one very spoiled Dalmatian. He is a certified trained chef and loves hosting great dinner parties.

ABOUT MARKETING MENTOR

Marketing-Mentor.com is a resource for creative professionals—by creative professionals—who want to grow their business. We help you focus on the business side of your creative business. We provide the tools you need. Then we point you in the right direction so you can do what needs to be done.

Working with both beginners as well as veteran creative professionals, we offer one-on-one coaching, training workshops and seminars through which we teach you everything you need to know about business growth, pricing and the art self promotion. We help you set realistic goals, show you how to reach them and then keep you on track until you do. With Marketing Mentor by your side, you'll learn how to make your creative business work for you.

At Marketing-Mentor.com, you will also find a growing resource of tools and educational products you can use to take your business to the next level. Visit www.marketing-mentor.com and be sure to sign up for the free half hour phone consultation—don't worry, it's not a sales pitch. It's just a way to get a taste of how Marketing Mentor can help you grow your business.

CONTACT US AT:

MARKETING MENTOR
P.O. Box 23, Hoboken, NJ 07030
Phone: (201) 653-0783, Fax: (201) 222-2494
Email: ilise@marketing-mentor.com
web site: www.marketing-mentor.com

CONTENTS

FOREWORD

This is a book about having fun.

What the… ?!? you're saying. *I thought this was a book about building my @#%* business! Is this some kind of bait and switch?*

No. It isn't.

Nevertheless, this *is* a book about having fun … with your business.

Because here's what I know: When I met Ilise Benun and Peleg Top, I was *not* having fun. I was a fledgling designer being buried alive by my nascent business—if by "business," you mean "a handful of clients who barely kept me in coffee and fonts." I was exhausted from trying to be everything to everybody and despondent about the prospects of changing my destiny.

Convinced that this was my own fault—I was a bad designer, I was too introverted to promote myself, I was missing the money-management gene—I landed on Peleg's doorstep a terrified wreck. In just under six hours, he managed not only to change my mind about my situation being hopeless, he actually got me excited about turning it around.

After getting the basic principles down—the very stuff you'll find in between the covers of this book—I signed on with Ilise, who helped me work them, bit by bit. Once again, what floored me was how much *fun* it was, creating (or re-creating) this business of mine. Naming it. Learning to connect with people. Figuring out creative, interesting ways to promote myself. Discovering that marketing didn't have to be something that made me sick to my stomach, but that actually *fed* me:

- I began enjoying myself at networking events, where—magically, it seemed—I began to pick up new clients who didn't flinch at real-world prices.

- Prospective clients started calling me—cold!

- I launched an electronic newsletter that not only went from 134 readers to almost 500 in under eight months, but that the guy who literally wrote the book on e-newsletters actually featured as a stellar example in his own e-newsletter.

I grew to enjoy the process of marketing so much, I ended up partnering with Ilise and Peleg to run The Marketing Mix, the official blog of Marketing Mentor.

Bottom line: I have lived virtually every word of this book, from the choosing of a market to growing your business by the admittedly counterintuitive (not to mention terrifying) process of firing bad clients, and I'm here to tell you, it works. When you work it, that is.

So make this your work. Take this book and work it to death. Start from the beginning, or jump to a subject you're grappling with now. Mark it up, highlight it, put sticky notes all over the danged thing, but dig in. The more you work it, the harder it will work for you.

And keep working it. If there's one thing I've learned from Ilise and Peleg, it's that marketing is an ongoing process. There's always some area of your business you'll need to be working on now. Keep this handy at your desk; if you're one of those over-workers (ahem!), take it with you to bed, in the tub, on vacation. There is no right or wrong way to use it, as long as you do use it.

There's one final thought I'll leave you with: For the love of all that's holy, have *fun* with this. Really. Sure, it's a little intimidating when you stare at the big, long list of stuff you're going to want to do to get your business firing on all cylinders. But if you break the process up into little pieces, it turns into sort of a mad, crazy and yes, really fun game. Because piece by piece, pixel by pixel, word by word, you'll be building the business of your dreams. A business that can grow as you grow, change as you change, support the dreams you started out with and lead you down wondrous paths you never imagined.

I'm serious.

But not *too* serious.

Peleg and Ilise wouldn't have it any other way.

 **COLLEEN WAINWRIGHT**
the communicatrix
December, 2007

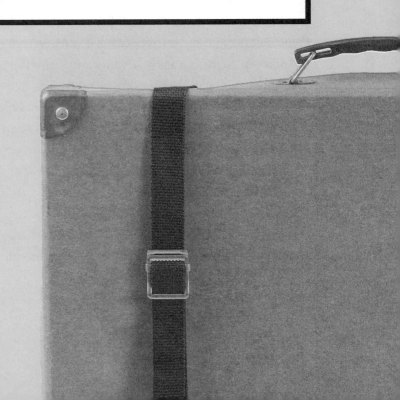

PART ONE

MARKETING

CHAPTER 1
WHO IS MY MARKET?

The beauty of being a designer is that almost every company, organization—even every person—could potentially use your services, because they all need to market themselves one way or another. Sometimes, all you have to do is tell people what you do and they say, "I know someone who needs a brochure or a web site or (fill in the blank)." In fact, once you open your eyes to all the sources of work, your biggest challenge will be deciding where to focus. But decide you must, because if you don't, you'll be all over the place in terms of your own marketing efforts and the client's perception of you will be muddy instead of clear.

That's why "everything must flow from the market." In other words, when you think about your business, don't start with "Who do I want to work with?" Instead, the question should be, "What does the market need and how can I satisfy that need while doing something I love?"

The specialty or niche you choose should be located at the intersection of two things: the needs of the marketplace and your services, skills and talents—in that order. You must align your specialty in response to the needs you perceive in the market-place. And don't specialize in something for which the need is on the wane. For example, it doesn't matter how much you know about widgets because their popularity is sinking fast, so you won't get any work. However, doohickeys are on the rise and might be worth promoting as one of your specialties.

The point is that a successful business is centered around a market and that market's needs. It's not centered around your wishes and desires. Ideally, what you want will overlap with what they need, but what you want should not be the source.

Likewise, don't rack your brain trying to come up with a company name or tagline. Instead, let that come from the market, too. Listen in such a way that you hear people's needs in everything they say. Then take the words they use to describe their problems or challenges and use the same words to describe how your services solve those problems. It's the difference between saying "I'm a web designer" and "I design clean and simple web sites for companies who want their visitors to stay on their site."

So how do you choose a market?

BUILD ON THE FOUNDATION OF YOUR EXPERTISE

The foundation of your business should be rooted strongly in something you know well and in which you already have some expertise. Whenever possible, don't start from scratch. Even if you're just starting out, it helps to build your business on something that already exists, such as past employment experience, a recent pro bono or side project, even a hobby. All of these can be used as springboards.

If you're making the transition from corporate work, even if you're sick of the field you are coming from, it's important to build on that investment, not just throw it away because of how you feel about it right now. You'll have a much easier time leveraging the relationships that you have already established and using the knowledge that you've acquired. Once you have a business under way, you can move toward new markets. But starting a business and approaching a new market simultaneously is double the work.

If you're leaving an industry precisely because there's absolutely no work there, then look for something peripherally related, something that will allow you to say honestly, "I'm familiar with this market." For example, if you worked for American Express, your potential markets might include the travel industry or financial services.

You must choose a focus, whether it's a horizontal focus ("I can design web sites for any company across the board") or a vertical focus ("I can design everything a real estate developer needs").

Sometimes this happens organically. Someone asks for your help, you do the project, you enjoy it, you do a good job, the client is satisfied, and you start wondering how you can use that experience to generate more like it.

Other times, you will have no choice but to start from scratch. You might say to yourself, "I want to work in the entertainment industry. It looks like a lot of fun and I think I would enjoy it," even if you have no experience, no contacts, nothing to build on. It's not impossible to build a business this way, but it does take longer. That you should know.

SPECIALIZING LETS YOU DOMINATE THE MARKET

Many designers believe that marketing the widest range of services to the largest possible group is the path to success. You'd rather be a generalist because you think you'll get more business. And on one level, it makes sense: The more opportunities you have to make a sale, the more sales you are likely to make. But in reality, it doesn't work that way. In fact, success comes to those who focus on the smallest number of activities most likely to yield the quickest and largest return.

It is tempting to position yourself broadly, thinking that a narrow focus will reduce the universe of available opportunities. But if you want to be credible, you must limit your offerings. Without some specialization, you would not be able to provide a coherent message to the marketplace, nor would you be able to qualify potential clients quickly, which leads to wasted time and effort.

We live in the era of the specialist. In fact, the larger your target market, the more you need to specialize. Being a generalist, trying to be all things to all people, doesn't sustain long-term business growth because you never create an identity and you never focus on a market that identifies you as their expert. Instead, you're a blur in the mind of your market.

Unlike a major design firm, you do not have limitless resources and a huge experience base in every facet of business. Specializing allows you to show the marketplace that you have a set of competencies that are focused enough to be done by a sole proprietor or small firm with a limited number of associates. Besides, your clients need to know that you not only understand the specific challenges that they face, but also that you have explicit experience that will help them. They don't want to be your guinea pigs.

In order to rise above the information overload that bombards your clients, you must distinguish yourself from all the other designers clamoring at your clients' doors. The only way to make a strong enough impact in the minds of your prospects so they choose you is to be clear about what you stand for: your focus or area of expertise.

And although corporations everywhere attempt to grow by expanding their offerings with spin-offs and line extensions, the majority of successful businesses—large corporations as well as small ones—succeed by sticking with a very narrow focus: on a market, on a product or service, on a benefit to the customer, on a single need of the customer, on a geographical location, on a category within a category, as well as on the marketing tools used to reach those customers.

If you still resist specializing, what you fail to understand is that your clients need you to specialize in exactly the service they need. They need to know they are dealing with an expert who serves their particular needs. That's what will make them feel more comfortable choosing you. That's what will help them sell you to their managers. So in reality, and in the long run, specializing gets you more business.

But focus doesn't come naturally. In fact, lack of focus does. Focus requires ongoing attention and discipline, which is why many people don't do it. It's not something you do once and then it's done. Focusing means committing, and then recommitting, to your plan every day, refocusing your attention and reevaluating your choices on a regular basis. That's the way to dominate the marketplace.

Here's what else you get when you specialize:

• **Fame:** You'll become known as an expert in your area of focus.

- **Fortune:** You'll command higher fees for your expertise.
- **Choice:** You'll get the work you want instead of taking whatever comes along.
- **Success:** You'll achieve your personal and business goals.

FOUR STRATEGIES FOR SPECIALIZING

1. Start out broad and evolve your specialty.

If you are a new designer, you may be a generalist simply because you don't yet know what to specialize in. That's fine, but as you begin to work with your clients, be attentive to what they are asking for and what they seem to need without knowing it. Then start giving it to them. Ask yourself questions like: "Of all the services I offer, which one is being requested most often? What do people seem to be the most perplexed about? What new technology do people need to understand?"

Anticipate the needs of your clients, and evolve your business to satisfy those needs. Start focusing your services and proclaiming your specialty as soon as you can. It will snowball. The more you talk about it, the better the response, which gives you more opportunities to learn more about and reinforce your specialty.

2. Focus on an industry and offer it multiple services.

Focusing on a vertical industry allows you to market yourself the most efficiently. You will get to know the industry and the people in the industry, who will talk to each other and spread the word about you. You can join the main trade organizations and use the member directories, which means that your list of prospects can be found all in one place. You can speak at conferences sponsored by the industry to increase your visibility and credibility. You can get your articles printed in online and offline trade publications for maximum exposure.

In addition, you'll be able to make the most powerful statement to your clients: "I really know your business." Nothing has a stronger impact. You will become an expert not only in your business, but also in their business, which becomes one of your most important benefits to your clients. As you get to know them, as you watch their industry grow and change, you also evolve your services to change with the industry, adding and subtracting services as needed. By letting the growth flow from the needs of your clients, you grow your business organically, which makes less work for you.

3. Focus on a special skill or talent you have that fits a very specific need.

You also can approach your specialty from the opposite perspective: identify your skills and talents, and then approach the prospects who may need them. This is much less efficient because it means you have to repeat the same message, or a slightly revised version of the same message, to different industries over and over again. It's hard to build momentum when you're spinning many different plates, so this is not the ideal strategy. But if you are expert in your particular skill—for example, web design or annual report design—and you are willing to do extra marketing of your own services, then take that as your specialty.

4. Focus on companies of a certain size.

A company's challenges often are a function of its size. Small-business owners face different challenges than Fortune 500 companies. They have different budgets, different processes and more (or fewer) layers of bureaucracy. You can market to a variety of industries if you specialize in the challenges faced by companies of a particular size.

IT HELPS TO HAVE MORE THAN ONE AREA OF EXPERTISE

Specializing doesn't have to limit you to that one area. In fact, the ideal situation is to have two areas of specialty. Then, if your particular niche becomes the epicenter of an economic downturn, you have the flexibility and the agility to shift gears and pursue another avenue.

You also will probably be called upon by prospects to provide services that fall outside your skill set or your industry expertise. Then it's your choice, on a case-by-case basis, whether to take the work. This decision often will depend on how hungry you are, what's currently on your plate, what projects are pending and which prospects you are pursuing. The important thing is to be honest with your prospects about your skills in terms of their needs. They may have heard such good things about you that they want you anyway. Or maybe they are in a time crunch and are willing to take the chance. But put the ball in their court and let them decide whether to hire you.

Working outside your area of expertise, however, will take more time and effort on your part. You may not have the time or the desire to educate clients so their expectations are in order, or to learn enough about their industry to speak knowledgeably.

So now that you know why it's so important to choose a market, it's time to do so.

DEFINE YOUR MARKET

The goal of this exercise is to end up with three niche markets to explore. From there, you will whittle them down to one or two, based on the results of your initial marketing efforts. But you have to start with at least ten market ideas to get down to the final one or two.

With all of that in mind, list (in the table below) up to ten markets or groups of people who could use your services. Start with markets you know best, and then move on to markets you've dreamed about. Be as specific as possible, focusing on groups and subgroups of prospects.

For each market, indicate (in just a few words) why you think it's a good market for you. Then mark if you have, or could easily create, samples or something to present to this market to demonstrate that you know what they need.

MARKET	WHY	SAMPLES?
EXAMPLES		
Small service businesses	They need promo materials	X
Hairdressers	My cousin was one	
Software developers	I'm married to one	X
1.		
2.		

MARKET	WHY	SAMPLES?
3.		
4.		
5.		
6.		
7.		
8.		
9.		
10.		

Now, whittle the list of ten down to three of the best, most feasible markets for you.

1.	
2.	
3.	

For each of these three, do some research (on the Internet, asking people you know, etc.) to find out all you can about how viable it is as a market for you.

TARGET MARKET #1:

a. How many prospects are there (locally, nationally, globally)?

b. What is the average project or purchase size or value?

c. How often would they need your services per year?

TARGET MARKET #2:

a. How many prospects are there (locally, nationally, globally)?

b. What is the average project or purchase size or value?

c. How often would they need your services per year?

```
┌─────────────────────────────────────────────┐
│  ┌───────────────────────────────────────┐  │
│  │          TARGET MARKET #3:            │  │
│  │                                       │  │
│  ├───────────────────────────────────────┤  │
│  │                                       │  │
│  │ a. How many prospects are there       │  │
│  │    (locally, nationally, globally)?   │  │
│  │                                       │  │
│  ├───────────────────────────────────────┤  │
│  │ b. What is the average project or     │  │
│  │    purchase size or value?            │  │
│  │                                       │  │
│  ├───────────────────────────────────────┤  │
│  │ c. How often would they need your     │  │
│  │    services per year?                 │  │
│  │                                       │  │
│  └───────────────────────────────────────┘  │
└─────────────────────────────────────────────┘
```

IS THIS MARKET READY FOR YOU?

Now, of those three, choose one market to go after first. You may have trouble deciding on just one, but you must. You'll be happy you did, because you'll begin to see the results of your targeted efforts.

What is the market you've chosen?

Before you go looking for clients, get an overview of the state of this market. A little more research is in order:

- What is the current state of this market? Is it in a growth mode? If so, it may be a good time to enter. If not, you might be better off waiting and watching until things turn around.

- What size and what types of projects are available through this market? Are they the kind of projects that you enjoy and are capable of doing? Or do the projects conflict with the kind of work you normally do?

- Do the people in this market know they need your services? You may perceive a need or see a group as a perfect market for your services, but if the market itself doesn't perceive that need, it isn't worth your time trying to convince them.

- Are there other service providers like you already serving this market? If not, there may be a good reason. Maybe there's no need. Or maybe this market doesn't want to pay for services like yours. This is a very important piece of information that can save you a lot of time, so find out as much as you can. It may require attending an event or two and asking questions, or calling a couple people you find online.

- Do you like the people? Underneath it all, business is about people. If you don't get along with the people that make up the industry you've decided to target, you won't have it easy. For example, if you are a people person and you want to approach the software industry, which (we could generalize) is populated by computer programmers, many of whom are uncomfortable around people, then this might not be the market for you. But that is something you should decide once you've met a few of them first.

The point is that you are in the driver's seat here. It's your business, so why not choose a market that you want to work with and people you get along with?

GETTING WORK FROM YOUR FORMER EMPLOYER

If you've gone out on your own because you've been laid off or left your job for some other reason, it's likely that the company you worked for needs your services. Your inside intelligence, coupled with your existing network of contacts at the company, will help you land those first contracts that are so important to your early success. Here are some dos and don'ts on how to get work from your former employer:

- Do capitalize on your network. Maintain contacts in various departments and organizations. Don't let those relationships falter just because you're not on-site with them anymore. Call and e-mail regularly to let them know what you're doing and to find out how they're doing. Probe, in particular, for needs that you can help satisfy. Also, follow your contacts wherever they go. They may move on to other employers, so keeping in touch gives you a foot in the door with a brand new prospect.

- Do maximize your knowledge of the company's needs. Don't forget that you have a leg up because you know this company—its strengths and weaknesses, its motivations, its needs and its goals. Most important, you know how best to fulfill these needs.

- Don't wait for your former employer to come up with projects for you. Take a proactive approach by pitching ideas based on what you know and what you learn as you keep in touch.

- Don't sell yourself short. Former employers may expect your hourly rate simply to be your former hourly rate. They may not realize that you are now paying your own benefits, taxes and overhead.

INTRODUCING YOURSELF TO A BRAND NEW MARKET

Growing your design business is a lot like spinning plates. You should have one or two smoothly spinning in the air before turning your attention to a new one. You can't forget any of them, or they'll come crashing down when you're not paying attention. And it may take some time to get a new one spinning as smoothly as the first couple, so you have to give it a little spin on a regular basis.

Once you've got things under way in a sector you are familiar with and are on your way to establishing a solid reputation, you will want to expand into other markets in order to grow your business and provide new challenges for yourself. Or maybe you feel stuck in a rut in a specific industry, or that you've exhausted your options within a particular market, so it's time to introduce yourself to a new one.

Either way, know in advance that introducing yourself to a brand new market takes time and effort. Although it is something you may be forced to do because you're just starting out, it is best done parallel to marketing efforts already in progress in the market (or markets) where you have a foothold.

So where do you start?

Step 1: Do your research.

Find the major players in your industry of choice. Read industry publications. Make phone calls. Attend industry events to see if what you believe about that industry is, in fact, true. (Often, it isn't.) Search out other designers who are already working in the industry and find out what the environment is like for them. Don't approach them from a competitive point of view. Instead, approach with questions, from a research point of view as if (and this may be true) you are considering entering the market but are not sure yet whether you should. Approach them for help and ask what their business is like. Is there room for more? Is the industry expanding or diminishing? Is this a good time to enter that particular industry? Some may not be willing to share information with you, but you will certainly find someone who is, so keep looking.

Step 2: Attend a few events.

Continue doing your research and interviewing people you meet to find out what the industry is like, whether this industry works with outside designers, whether it's a close-knit industry and therefore difficult to break into or whether they are open to new resources. These are questions you can't answer by surfing a web site or reading a newsletter. That's why making contact with actual members of the market is essential. It will provide you with information and valuable insights you wouldn't even know to look for otherwise.

Step 3: Join the trade group.

Once you have done your research and decided this is the industry for you, find the market's trade organization and join it. If there are several groups to choose from, find out which is most active, has the best reputation and draws the specific people you need to meet. For example, in the cable industry, there are several groups (such as Women in Cable & Telecommunications, National Association of Broadcasters and National Association of Minorities in Communications), but only one that brings together marketing people in the cable industry—Cable & Telecommunications Association for Marketing. That's obviously the one to join if you are looking for the marketing people.

Likewise, the software industry boasts many different trade groups catering to the industry, but a designer would be best served by joining the one that addresses software marketing issues rather than a general software group. Or look for the special interest group (SIG) within an organization that focuses on your interest.

If you can't find a trade group for the market you've chosen, you should seriously consider choosing another market. If there is no trade association dedicated to it, it may not be a serious market, and therefore not worth your time. If there's no group that has a line of communication to your prospects—i.e., the people who buy your services—or that organizes events for your prospects through which you can meet them in person, your marketing workload will multiply tremendously.

Step 4: Introduce yourself to the leaders of the group.

Let them know who you are, what you do and that you want to be involved. Ask what opportunities are available for you to interact with your prospects. Find out whether you can teach a workshop, conduct a teleseminar, submit an article for their online and offline publications or sponsor an event. Don't be shy and secretive about why you are joining the group. There is nothing shameful about wanting to promote your services to them. After all, they just may have a need for them.

Step 5: Get the member directory and use it to make cold calls.

Many trade groups are turning their offline directories into online-only directories, but no matter the format, be sure to use this list of qualified prospects to make your cold calls. Warm up the call a bit by introducing yourself as a fellow member of the organization; let your prospects know where you got their names, and then tell them why you're calling. People are more responsive when there is a connection between the two of you, and this is your connection.

Step 6: Get involved in the life of the group.

Don't think that the new clients will pour in simply because you send in your dues and read the monthly e-mail newsletter.

Once you've determined that this is the market for you, you must get involved in the life of that market. Here are some suggestions for how to do so:

- Attend a board meeting to find out what the group is doing.

- Attend an educational event to find out what kinds of people attend the events—even if the meeting topic isn't of particular interest to you. For example, you may join the American Marketing Association (AMA) with the assumption that you'll easily find marketing directors of corporations at their meetings. However, many of the AMA chapter events are attended by consultants and owners of market research firms, most of whom are also looking for prospects. This means you'll have to do a little more digging to find out where and how to meet your actual prospects. Maybe they attend the annual conferences or participate on the listserv operated by the trade group. Or maybe they're listed in the group's directory. This information is not readily available, and you may need to develop a relationship with someone at the organization in order to find it out.

- Volunteer to be on a committee. People get to know each other by working together on projects, which is why trade associations are the perfect vehicle for getting to know new prospects. The structure is already in place for you; all you have to do is make the effort to work within it. It's crucial that your prospects see you work. So find out what needs to be done, especially as it relates to your expertise, and then volunteer to do it. For example, if the group needs someone to design a web site or an invitation for a conference, raise your hand. Choose tasks that will bring you into contact—ideally in person—with other members, members of the press or bigwigs in the industry. This can be an excellent door opener and can put you in the vicinity of people who wouldn't otherwise take your call.

CREATING SAMPLES FOR A NEW MARKET

If you're just starting out, or if you want to introduce your services to a new market, you need samples to show these new prospects—but you need to have clients in order to create the samples, right?

Well, there are three techniques you can use to get around this catch-22:

- Offer to do work at a reduced rate for friends or networking buddies so that you can build your portfolio.

- Whenever you see design that you think you could do better, simply create that better example on your own dime. Then reach out to the company, tell them what you've done and offer to show it to them. That's something they will probably want to see. They become an automatic prospect for whom you have customized your portfolio. (By the way, don't confuse this marketing technique with "spec" work, where the client asks you to work for free to test you out.)

- Offer to do a free critique of a prospect's existing materials. That way, you can show what you know in a way that's directly related to your prospect, rather than show what you've done for others.

FINDING THE IDEAL CLIENT

If you find yourself complaining about your clients because they don't treat you right or don't pay your bills on time, you may need to get some new ones. No problem; if you're marketing yourself regularly, clients are a dime a dozen.

The trick to finding good ones is knowing what you want. So take a moment now to daydream a bit and determine who your ideal client is.

List three types of people or companies that you most effectively help.

1.

2.

3.

List the kinds of problems you help these people solve.

Describe your ideal client—in particular, the person's personality traits that you like. Include how the client treats you.

What is the best thing about your ideal client?

What is the ideal project that your ideal client would bring you?

What does your ideal client understand about the way you work?

What would your ideal client never do?

Now, with this profile in mind, go out looking for your ideal client. You'll be surprised how many you'll find.

CHAPTER 2
HOW CAN I FIND CLIENTS AND PROSPECTS?

You've done your research, you've narrowed it down and you've chosen your market. Your next step is to find that market. Until now, this target market has just been an abstract group; now you're going to put names and phone numbers and e-mail addresses (and eventually faces, we hope) to that group.

Here's how: Go where they go, read what they read, find out what lists they are on and use all that information to reach out to them.

RESEARCHING YOUR MARKET

For the people in your chosen market, find out:

Where do they go? What trade groups do they belong to? What conferences do they attend? Where do they meet for education or networking? List five different places you might find them in person (or online):

1.

2.
3.
4.
5.

What magazines and trade publications do they read? What web sites and blogs do they visit and rely on? What newsletters and e-zines do they read? What listservs or e-mail lists do they subscribe to and maybe even go to for help? List five publications (both online and offline) read by your market:

1.
2.
3.
4.
5.

What lists are they on? What lists and directories are available to reach them? (These could be related to trade groups they belong to or magazines they read.) Name five of these lists:

1.	
2.	
3.	
4.	
5.	

HOW TO FIND EVENTS TO ATTEND

There are many events to attend—too many, actually. Too many ways to meet people you'll never see again, too many opportunities to collect a stack of business cards you'll never look at again. Those are wasted networking efforts.

The key is to choose your events carefully, and then be sure to have a follow-up system.

You can find out about local events through a local newspaper or through Internet listings that publish local events. Almost every town has a business paper that lists events. You also can do an Internet search for "name of town" + "business events" to see what comes up. Your first step is to make sure you start each week by looking at the events taking place and choosing one (or more) to attend.

Here are some other sources for events:

- local libraries
- business newspapers and journals
- trade groups with local chapters
- general event listings
- web sites
- e-mail newsletters that send out regular event announcements

You'll find all sorts of events, from local Rotary Club and chamber of commerce meetings to city council meetings and local charity events. All are potential places for you to meet your prospects, depending on who your prospects are.

You're probably also familiar with events put on by your own trade group, events where you will meet people offering the same basic services as you. For designers, there are local chapters in the United States for the Graphic Artists Guild or the AIGA. The event topics from these groups may be of interest to you, and the relationships you can cultivate there are worthwhile because you need the support and resources of your colleagues—and sometimes they even pass work along—but you won't find your prospects there.

If you're going to get new clients, you have to find a group of prospects. So if the market you've chosen is small-business owners, you'll probably find them at business card exchanges put on by the chamber of commerce or at weekly Business Networking International meetings. (BNI is one of several networking groups with local meetings all over the world, so you will likely find one in your area to explore.)

If you market to financial services companies, then you need to find groups like Financial Women's Association or Financial Communications Society.

If you don't specialize in a niche, it will be very difficult to find good networking opportunities where you can meet your prospects; your networking efforts will therefore be scattershot and inefficient.

Business card exchanges and other networking events are high-pressure situations where people go to meet others, but usually do so with all their defenses intact. For more relaxed networking, try educational environments, such as workshops and seminars, where the focus is on learning.

Which Events Should You Attend?

Once you've got your list of possible events, here are three questions to help you decide which ones to attend:

- Does the topic address an issue your prospects and clients face? If so, then go. And bring back some ideas for them.

- Do you want to meet the speakers? If so, then go. And be sure to introduce yourself at the end, get their business cards and follow up later with "I heard you speak." It's a sure way to get a conversation going.

- Does the event relate to a new idea you haven't had time to focus on, something you want to learn about or expand your business into? If so, then go. And use it as a catalyst to get the ball rolling.

Which Groups Should You Join?

Most of the educational and networking events are sponsored by a group that you could belong to—and you should, especially if it's one where you'll find prospects.

But before you join an organization or decide if you are going to continue with the ones you're already in, here are five questions to answer:

1. Do your interests match the organization?
2. Are important prospects and referral sources active in the organization?
3. Are your current contacts active in the organization?
4. Are there opportunities to showcase your abilities?
5. Are your competitors already active there, and would there be room for you?

If so, by all means, join and participate. But don't do it impulsively. Take your time making a decision and be sure to join a group to which you can make a commitment of time. Otherwise, it's a waste. You might as well simply attend a meeting here or there.

Which Trade Shows Should You Attend?

Trade shows are great because lots of people (ideally, your prospects) in one industry come together under one roof, making it a potentially rich marketing opportunity. Exhibiting at these events can be very costly, though, and it isn't always the best way to make contact with your prospects. If your prospects are the vendors at the trade show, don't get a booth for yourself because you won't be able to walk the floor and meet them. However, if your prospects are the attendees, it makes sense to exhibit so that a steady stream of potential clients will come by your booth to chat with you. Either way, go as an attendee the first year to scope it out.

What Should You Do at Trade Shows?

Janet Ryan, a trade show marketing specialist, writes: "Good prospectors never miss a chance to attend events specific to their industry or the events prospects are likely to be attending. But wandering the halls in the hope of running into a good prospect is an inefficient and unprofessional way to approach the task."

Instead, you should print out an exhibitor list (if available) and spend a little time scanning the web sites of the companies in attendance. Then, use that information to decide which prospects you most want to speak with and identify names of the key contacts. You should know enough about their products or services to have an intelligent conversation with staff members in the booth. But don't be too talkative. Remember that they are at the show to sell, not to hear your pitch, so respect their time and talk about their businesses more than yours. And if you see a prospect for *their* business hovering around waiting to speak with them, excuse yourself so they can sell. It will be appreciated.

If you can't get an exhibitor list beforehand, you have to be a bit more ingenious. Arrive early and pick up the on-site exhibitor list or just walk around building your own. Then, duck out to the nearest Starbucks (or other wireless hotspot) and do the same online research as if you had the list beforehand. It'll cost you an hour or two away from the event, but it will make your experience far more productive and get you a lot further along in building fruitful relationships.

ASKING FOR (AND GETTING) REFERRALS

BY PELEG TOP

At the beginning of every year, I plan the marketing of my business, Top Design, for the next twelve months. Last year, when I took a closer look at the previous year's sales, I realized that although I do fine with traditional marketing tools (such as direct mail, web site and e-mail), most of the good clients came from referrals. And when it wasn't a direct referral, what I usually heard was "I heard about your firm from so and so," although I had no idea who "so and so" was.

The fact was, people were talking. Work was coming in. My clients were sharing their good experiences with their friends, which resulted in business growth for Top Design. Word of mouth was happening without me doing a thing. It was like discovering that I had a goldmine under the house and never knew about it. But I wondered, if this was happening without any action on my part, what could happen if I got a little more active about it? That's when I saw a great opportunity to grow my business by asking for referrals instead of passively waiting for them to come to me.

My first step was to identify the people who were most likely to refer my firm to others. According to *The Anatomy of Buzz* by Emanuel Rosen, friends and relatives are the number-one source of information for referrals. So I took a closer look at my Rolodex and identified the top twelve clients who have become good friends. I only chose clients who provided the best work with the largest budgets. It was their circle of friends I wanted to tap into. The list was short but powerful.

Since the year was just starting, I planned the first phase of this "referral marketing campaign" to start in February, on Valentine's Day to be exact. I had less than four weeks to come up with something that would make my clients want to open their Rolodexes. So my team and I got out of the office and went to the local mall to see what could inspire us to create an interesting marketing piece.

We walked out of the mall with twenty oversized Chinese take-out boxes and twenty pounds of Hershey's Kisses. We knew that no one could resist chocolate!

Next on our list was creating the "asking vehicle" for the referrals. We designed a custom greeting card that read "Refer Your Love" on the front. Inside, the personalized card told the clients how much we enjoy working with them, thanked them for their business and asked them for names of a few people who might enjoy our services. We included a self-addressed response card (yes, using old-fashioned snail mail) so they could give us names and contact info for their friends.

We delivered our packages by messenger on Valentine's Day.

Within a week, the response cards started coming back. Of the twelve we sent out, we received six back. That's a 50 percent return!

Of the six cards that we received, we got twelve referrals to new prospects. From those twelve, we cultivated eight relationships and closed approximately $160,000 in business in the next two months.

Our cost? $330, which included messenger services to deliver each package.

Sometimes you have to ask for the business rather than wait for it to come to you. My clients were happy to share their contacts with me, and I am sure they thought of me every time they bit into the chocolates I sent. That's a sweet place to be.

HOW TO MEET PROSPECTS WHO AREN'T GEOGRAPHICALLY CLOSE TO YOU

It used to be that your market was limited by your geographical location or the resources you had (or didn't have) to travel to visit your prospects and clients. Not anymore. These days, you can work with anyone almost anywhere across the globe, thanks to the Internet and the technology to work virtually.

Another change has taken place in the mindset of business people. Before the Internet, prospects would only work with designers they could meet in person. Now, there is much more acceptance of working with vendors you may have only spoken to on the phone, provided that the trust is there; this is why building trust during the marketing process is essential.

There will still be people who prefer to work with a local designer, and you won't be able to convince them otherwise. But if, in your marketing efforts, you focus on those who are open to working virtually, you'll find them.

Reaching beyond your geographic area might be important because you live in a small town with very few design needs, or because the work available isn't the work you want to do, or because the local fees paid for the work you do is lower than what you'd like to earn. Go virtually to where the work is. Don't assume prospects around the country won't be interested just because you're not in their neighborhood. Play up the fact that they won't have to waste time meeting with you and that, if necessary, you will come to meet with them.

When approaching national prospects, you will have to use different marketing tools than you would if your prospects were local. For example, you won't be able to do as much in-person networking if their trade group meets monthly in another state. However, you can attend an annual conference or trade show, then follow up by phone, e-mail, snail mail and any other new-fangled tool that comes along.

It will take more work on your part to pursue these prospects, but it will be worth the effort.

USING MAILING LISTS

It may seem obvious, but when you introduce yourself to a new market, the most important tool at your disposal is a list of your prospects. Without that list, there's very little you can do.

With that list, there is much you can do. You can make cold calls. You can send personalized e-mail messages. You can do a mailing of your brochure or promotional package. Or, you can do all of the above. In other words, you can use that list for a campaign. (More about that in Chapter Four.)

Where Do These Lists Come From?

There are many resources for a list of prospects, especially if you don't need thousands of prospects. But the most effective list is generally one you create yourself, based on the criteria you've chosen, such as the size of the company, possible revenue or the number of employees. Although it requires a bit more work on your part, compiling and collecting names for your own list will make for a much more effective and profitable list.

Be wary of someone selling "prospect lists" because although they sound good and are often very inexpensive, the people on the list may be someone's prospects, but they usually are not yours.

You probably have access to lists that you may not be aware of, so look first to your own resources, which may include:

- Industry and trade group directories. Almost every trade group publishes a directory, either online or printed. As a member of a group, one of the benefits you get is access to (and inclusion in) the member directory. (Some groups make their directories available for a fee, so you don't even have to join.) You may not realize it, but this is one of the most valuable resources and best reasons to join a group. Directories are invaluable because they pre-qualify your prospects and give you the name of someone to start with, which saves your valuable time. Calling a company and trying to find the person who hires or buys the services you're offering is very time-consuming.

- Attendee lists to industry events. Often, a list of attendees will be published and distributed to attendees of an industry event or conference—it's one of the perks of attending. This is another invaluable resource that you should do more than just glance at to see who's in attendance. Make this list your bible. At the event, use it to find the people you want to talk to. Get familiar with the names. Mark it up. Write notes to yourself about who you met, as well as who you didn't meet but can follow up with later. Then, when you get home, use that list. Make cold calls using the conference as your connection. If you didn't meet the person you are contacting, your opening line when you call or e-mail could be, "We both attended the AMA meeting last night but we didn't have a chance to meet, so I thought I'd call and find out a bit about what you do." That connection usually makes them open to listening or reading further. (There is usually a caveat not to use the list for "mass marketing," but you can use it to make contact with people.)

- Resource lists published in trade publications. Many trade publications offer (usually around year-end) annual lists of the top players in a particular industry, complete with contact information and details about the products and services offered by the company. This is not only a great source of prospects, but also a good overview of an industry that you may be considering getting into.

Should You Rent a List?

Any list broker can rent you any of the more than 30,000 commercially available lists. But renting a list won't necessarily make your marketing profitable. The minimums are high (generally 5,000), and you just don't need that many names to work with.

There are lists available specifically for businesses targeting marketing communications prospects. These lists are best if you're willing to pay for someone else to provide the names and contact information for prospects because it saves you a lot of time. Start small, with 100 or 250 good prospects, to get your marketing going.

Many designers buy or subscribe to these lists but don't get much out of them. They may do one mailing, get very little return and proclaim the list worthless. It's not the list's fault; it's the designer's. The list is just one spoke on the marketing wheel. Use the list to develop relationships with these prospects, communicate with them consistently over time, and your efforts will be successful.

You've no doubt received e-mail messages offering e-mail lists with millions of names. Well, don't do it, ever. Not only is using these lists considered spamming, but these lists are not qualified for your purposes. The chances that your prospects are on them are one in a million—not great odds.

ONLINE LISTS OF MARKETING COMMUNICATIONS PROSPECTS

www.thelistonline.com

www.adbase.com

www.creativeaccess.com

www.blackbook.com

www.hoovers.com

HOW TO BUILD YOUR DREAM LIST

How much would you pay for a list of people who need your services—and know it—and who are so close to being ready to buy that they've already made the effort to contact you? Wouldn't that be worth a lot of money? Might it even be invaluable?

The best list for you is the list of people with whom you have already begun the process of building a relationship. Don't underestimate its value for a minute, even if the list is small. These people already know you, and may even trust you (at least more than those on the mailing list you're thinking of renting), which means that the amount of time it will take to make the sale is shorter.

There are two strategies for building your dream list: First, you choose your prospects by compiling names from e-mail messages lingering in your inbox, old invoices, business cards, attendee lists from networking meetings and little bits of paper strewn about your office (you know the ones). The names you want to capture are quite simply those of everyone who's ever expressed interest in your work.

While you're building that list, also be using marketing tools that motivate qualified leads to raise their hands and ask you to market to them—tools like e-mail newsletters, publicity and press coverage, a toll-free number and offers of free info.

Sound like a lot of work? It's actually not the complex task you may imagine it to be—it just takes some work and some time. In fact, compiling your dream list is an ongoing process that can be surprisingly economical and made to fit manageably into your day-to-day routine. Just keep your eyes open and be organized about it.

The people who take precious time out of their days to respond to an offer you make do so for a reason: They have a need. These people are your hot prospects, and they've qualified themselves. They've raised their hands and said, "I need what you have. Please tell me more." Whether they know it or not, they've granted you permission to market to them.

CHERRY-PICKING PROSPECTS

One of the benefits of being small is that you don't need hundreds of clients, so you can afford to target your market very specifically. That means instead of reaching out to thousands of nonprofit organizations, you can choose the ten or twenty-five or fifty you want to work with and go after them. In reality, most of the companies you pursue won't have a need for your services at the moment you approach them (although a few might). But if you initiate a relationship now, and start getting to know them and letting them get to know you, down the road, when they do have a need, the foundation will already be set, the trust established, and you'll be a shoo-in.

Reach out to people you read about in a trade journal or local online news source. Always keep your eyes open for the choice prospects whose names you come across in a magazine article here and there. Write them a letter, send them an e-mail or just pick up the phone and call to introduce yourself. This is a cold call, yes, but what makes this kind of cold call instantly warm is the feeling behind your response, your genuine interest in this company. It's very flattering to your prospect (providing it's true, of course) to hear that you are calling because you have chosen them based on what you know, what you've seen and what you have to offer. If there really is a fit that you can describe clearly, they just might agree to meet you. And that may well develop into a lucrative and productive working relationship, either now or later.

Now that you're clear on the market you will be pursuing, you can turn your focus inward. Looking at your own services within the context of the market you're pursuing will make your marketing much easier.

CHAPTER 3
HOW SHOULD I PRESENT MYSELF?

It's not just corporations that need to brand themselves. Individuals and small firms need to stand out from the crowd, too. Establishing a brand involves developing recognition, preference, loyalty and trust among prospects and those who count in the industries in which you focus. This isn't about spin-doctoring; it's about being clear about what you have to offer, conveying that message concisely, then positioning yourself in relationship to the needs of your prospects.

A brand is more than an image, and hype will take you only so far. You must back up your brand with substance and value.

Regardless of the size of your company, whether it's just you or you and a large group of people, your prospects and clients need to know that they're working with professionals. There are many small things—activities and behaviors and marketing tools—that contribute to your "personal brand." These small things are what clients see and then use to make their decisions about whether to work with you. So the more consistent your message and image across all these elements are, the more confidence prospects have in you and the easier their decision will be.

WHY YOU MUST HAVE A PERSONAL BRAND

At the end of the day, most people won't understand or remember the details of what you do. That's fine. All you want is for them to associate a simple idea with your name or company name. So for us, "Ilise does marketing and self-promotion for creative types" or "Peleg is a designer, and I think he does a lot of special events" is enough, allowing anyone to pass our names along to someone who might need help with these services.

FINDING YOUR PERSONAL BRAND

Before you can convey any message to your market, you have to find that message. And before you can find the message, you not only have to understand the needs of your market, but you also have to understand yourself. That's the part of this process many people skip right past.

You may believe you know yourself just fine, or that there's not much to know. But in reality, each of us is a very complex individual who is constantly changing. So even if the questions on the next page are ones you've thought about before, it's quite possible you've changed since the last time you thought about them.

Take some time to think through these questions. Begin by reading through the exercise before you write down anything. Then go back and fill in your answers.

1. Why did you choose the design industry? How did you get involved?

2. What is it about design that you are passionate and excited about?

3. What are your three strongest and three weakest skills?

   1.

   2.

   3.

4. What are your three most positive and three most negative personality traits?

            Positive   Negative

   1.

   2.

   3.

5. How does your business best take advantage of your greatest skills and talents? How are you utilizing these skills and talents right now?

6. What new business skills have you learned in the past year?

7. What professional organizations are you associated with? What do you contribute to these groups?

8. What business or work success are you most proud of having accomplished?

9. What are the three most interesting things you have done or experienced in your life?

    1.

    2.

    3.

10. What obstacles have you overcome to get where you are today, both professionally and personally? What essential lessons have you learned from your mistakes?

THE NAME OF YOUR BUSINESS

Next, we'll turn toward your business and, in particular, what to call it. You may already have a business name, but if after reading this section you can see that it doesn't work from a marketing perspective, consider changing it.

The main objective to keep in mind is this: Your business name should convey information about your business. If it doesn't convey anything, it's essentially useless—unless you're Google and have gobs of money to spend teaching people a new word.

Naming a company is difficult when you're just starting out or making a transition. Your business will necessarily change and evolve as you begin to find your market and as you learn more about the needs of that market. If you choose a name at the very beginning, it may not reflect what you actually end up doing. It's kind of like building a web site: The first version is usually a simple one, but as a business grows, so does the web site.

It's the same for your business name. It must have room for growth, some of which you will be able to anticipate; other growth you can't possibly imagine—and that's one of the things that makes self-promotion fun and exciting. Your business can take you places you never thought you'd go. People will ask you to do things you never thought of doing, which will take you in a direction you hadn't anticipated. Your business name should, ideally, be able to transform and grow as your business grows, too.

So, if possible, start with something that is more general than specific, and consider it temporary. It might make sense to start with your name as the business name (read on for more about this). That, at least, is less likely to change.

The bottom line is this: Take your time. Don't rush into making a decision about your company name. If necessary, in the interim, use a simple business card with your personal name and a list of services you're offering. As you interact with people, especially with clients, it will become clearer what you're doing and what you should call your business.

This is where the mantra "Self-promotion is not about you" starts. You probably have lots of cute and clever ideas for a business name. But those are probably from your own point of view and not that of your clients. For example, a client recently had a consultation to discuss the naming of his business and his logo. As a designer, he was very focused on which logo looked better, but he had not given much thought to the name he'd chosen: John Smith Digital Graphics.

At networking events, he was dismayed to discover that no one understood what digital graphics meant. Many people thought he offered pre-press services (which he doesn't). When asked what tangible product his clients get as a result of working with him, he said, "They get a web site that is usable."

Oh, so he's a web site designer. Why didn't he just say that?

Partially because he doesn't want to say what everyone else says. He wants to be different. But this is neither the time nor the place to be different. Because if you present yourself using unclear words that confuse your prospects, they'll never turn into clients. They need to understand right away what they'll get from working with you. You can elaborate and fill in the details later.

Should Your Name Be Your Business Name, Too?

You may not realize it, but your name is more than just your name. It's also a valuable marketing tool at your disposal. So how should you use it?

One of your marketing objectives is to have a little share of your prospects' minds so that when a need arises, your name comes readily to them. If you've been working for any length of time, there is undoubtedly a reputation that precedes you—people who know you or know of you, stories people can tell about you—for better or worse. If that's the case, you can capitalize on the reputation, or "brand recognition," you've already built for yourself by including your name in the name of your business or company.

On the other hand, if no one has ever heard of you, calling your firm Betty Smith and Associates will convey no information at all to a prospect who sees or hears it—so that doesn't work as a marketing tool.

Keep in mind that, sometimes, besides your name, the name of your business will be the only thing your prospects see—on a business card, on your nametag, on a list of attendees at a meeting—and it should therefore reflect the focus of the work that you do, since you won't always be available to elaborate. In fact, your company name should be so clear that it speaks for itself.

So while Smith & Associates may have name recognition, it conveys no information about the kind of services offered, much less a specialty. It could just as easily be a law firm as a marketing firm, and any prospect who saw only Smith & Associates would have no clue, which means a lost opportunity for business.

Smith Communications is little bit better because it is more descriptive (we know the business has something to do with communication) but still general enough to encompass many services and client needs (it could include services such as graphic design, writing, public relations, marketing, almost anything). So this could be a good candidate for a temporary name. It could become an umbrella name for different specific services offered, where different divisions of one company will each eventually go by their more specific name.

But Smith Copywriting or Smith Design—or, even better, Smith Direct Mail Copywriting or Smith Web Design—is even more descriptive, so prospects needing these specific services would immediately know they'd found what they were looking for.

BUSINESS NAMING DOS AND DON'TS

- Do think long-term. When choosing a business name, choose something you can live with for three to five years. As your business evolves, you will see whether or how you need to change your name. Don't change it just because you get bored, though, because you'll lose all the brand equity you've built into that name.

- Don't get too fancy or creative with your name, especially if your market is on the conservative side, because your clients won't understand what you do. The name should be easy to pronounce and to remember, not esoteric or obscure.

- Do consider where you'll land in alphabetical listings. If you can use one of the early letters in the alphabet, do so.

- Do make sure the name you select has only positive associations. For example, Accurate Bookkeeping Services not only has positive associations, but it also would be near the top of an alphabetical listing. Joyous Media has positive associations, but it doesn't communicate what the business is.

- Don't choose something that has a personal or private meaning. Many people also use their geographic locations in their business names, which is good if the market would appreciate a local vendor.

But sometimes it only has a personal meaning, like Mountain View Graphics or 408 Group (because the street address is 408).

- Do create a name that reflects a need your market has. For example, you can guess the specialty of a company called Reach-Women. When clients who need to reach women hear that name, they'll respond immediately because the name reflects their need. Or how about Cross It Off Your List, an organizing and relocation company in New York City? Think about what your prospects need, and how that need can be finessed into a business name.

- Do make sure the name of your business rolls easily off the tongue in two to three syllables. You don't want a long, unpronounceable name that people will avoid saying. And make sure it is easy to spell, because that will make it easier to find in search engines and on the Internet. If prospects misspell your web address, they may never find you—but they may find your competition.

Take your time thinking about this and getting feedback from other people. Your company name is an important choice.

DON'T FORGET ABOUT YOUR DOMAIN NAME

Imagine your prospect sitting at the computer. Maybe she met you the day before and now has a moment to look you up online. You gave her your business card, but it's in her purse in the other room and she doesn't want to get up right now. What does she do to find you?

She could Google you—and she might. (Have you ever done this—Googled yourself? You should do it on a regular basis just to see what people find when they go looking for you. It could be an enlightening experience.)

She might also guess what your web address would be. What does she guess? Your name? Your company name?

Your web address (or domain name) should be what your prospects and clients would guess if they didn't know it and had to type something into the web address field.

Choosing a domain name is an integral part of the process of choosing a business name. It may be obvious, but, ideally, if the web version of your business name is available, they should be one and the same.

If your company name has your name in it, then so should your domain name. If your company name refers to the kind of work you do, then so should your domain name. It's essential that there be consistency between these elements, or your prospects will either become confused or just not make the extra effort to find you online.

If you don't have an official business name yet, then your first choice for your domain name should be to use your personal name.

In fact, no matter what, you should own a domain in your own name and just have it point to any site you put up. If your own name is a popular one and therefore not available, get something close, perhaps one that uses your middle initial or some variation on your name.

The first top-level domain, ".com," is entrenched in the vernacular of business. People assume that a .com is a business, and even when they guess, they're likely to start with .com, so try to get a .com if you can, even if you have to modify your business name slightly.

Here are some other things to consider when choosing a domain name:

- Don't hesitate to hyphenate if it will allow you to have the name that works best. However, if you've used hyphenation in your web address, you'll have to draw more attention to it as you tell people what it is, to make sure they don't miss that dash and find your competition instead.

- Add "the" or something neutral to the front of your company name to get an available domain name.

- Buy more than one—they're cheap. If you can't decide, buy a few and have them all point to the same site.

Your business name is likely to come from someone else, not from you thinking hard about it. So listen closely to your prospects and clients when you talk to them about what you do. They might just say a phrase or a couple of words that will hit you in a "Eureka" moment; when you hear those words, you'll say, "That's the name of my business!"

GENERATING NAME IDEAS

Now that you have some ideas about what to think about when you name your business, you'll have an opportunity to implement them to generate some initial name ideas. You should still be very open at this point in the process. Don't approach this exercise with a fixed idea of what you want your name to be. That will get in your way.

List five things your clients need; turn each of these needs into a possible name for your business.

1.
2.
3.
4.
5.

Find three to five companies that offer services and products similar to yours (this may be your competition). Search the Internet, the Yellow Pages and any other relevant directory your prospects might go to. List the names of those companies here, and analyze what does or doesn't work about each one.

1.
2.
3.
4.
5.

Based on the things that work well in the above companies' names, come up with three options for your company name.

1.	
2.	
3.	

Now, go out and get feedback from at least five people about the three options for your company name. Make sure you approach a range of different types of people—not just friends and family, but also clients and prospective clients. Some should know what you do already; some shouldn't. Say, "If I said my company is called 'X,' what would you think I did for a living, or what assumptions will you make about my business?" Ask them to vote on your options, and also ask them for their ideas of variations on the names you've proposed or any other ideas they have. Be open to any ideas that come along.

Once you've gotten feedback, ask the following questions about each name that seems like a potential choice:

- Is it clear?
- Is it clever?
- Does it have impact?
- Does it include a solution to your clients' problems?
- Does it indicate a specialty?
- Does it name the audience or target market?
- Does it use positive language?
- Does it include any benefits?
- Does it use strong words?

WINNING TAGLINES TAKE THE
MYSTERY OUT OF YOUR SERVICES

So you've got a name for your company, which, when prospects hear or see it, will certainly offer a clue into the work you do. But, because of its required brevity, it won't convey much more than that. That's why you need a tagline.

Your tagline is a sentence or phrase that is memorable and easy to understand. The objective of your tagline is to convey the essence of your business in a nutshell.

The more specific your tagline can be, the better. Many business owners make the mistake of thinking that they'll be casting a wider net by being a generalist. They like "Providing all types of design services for all types of businesses" because it leaves out no one. But it will not leave prospects feeling confident that you understand their particular sector. A retailer prefers to work with a designer who specializes in retailers. A multi-channel retailer will prefer to work with a designer who specializes in that even narrower niche.

You may attract leads using a general tagline, but many of the leads will not be appropriate for you, and you will waste your time and theirs weeding through them. It's a common mistake to think that more leads are better, but chasing poor leads is very expensive, particularly if you're in a business where converting leads into sales often takes an investment of many (unpaid) hours of follow-up and in-person meetings.

That's where your tagline comes in; it can save you lots of time by helping the appropriate prospects see that you're just perfect for them, and the inappropriate prospects realize you're not what they need.

Here are some taglines examples:

- "We Get You Noticed!"
- "Graphic and Web Design With a Touch of Green"
- "Effective Results for All Your Trade Show Needs"
- "Combining Graphic Design & Project Management Into One Package"
- "Smart Design For Intelligent Businesses"
- "Design For Artists, Entrepreneurs and Other Creative Types"

CREATE A WINNING TAGLINE

Now you're ready to create your own tagline. Taglines often benefit from an iterative process of reconsideration. Don't engrave the first one you settle on into anything. You'll probably end up refining it based on something you hear or read. And you may find that some ideas from other exercises in this section fit into this exercise as well, so feel free to repeat or reuse that information.

What solution do you offer?

What is the end result of your services?

Why do clients hire you?

How do you solve the clients' problems?

What are your specific tactics?

Who is your audience? Specifically, what size business, what industry, what vertical niche?

Complete the formula for what you do.

What you do:

How you do it:

For whom:

So they can achieve what goal?

You probably selected the most polished way to complete each part of the formula above. Rephrase each section using common vernacular. Think of the slangiest way to say it.

What you do:

How you do it:

For whom:

So they can achieve what goal?

Would reversing the order help make the tagline fit better into conversation? Try moving the parts around.

For whom:

So they can achieve what goal?

What you do?

How you do it?

Is there a better way to say that? Can you turn the verb in the first part of the tagline into a gerund? For example, "How to acquire new customers for less" becomes "Acquiring new customers for less."

Now open a thesaurus. Are there more powerful verbs you can use? Try to select verbs with emotional baggage. If you're helping customers avoid something bad, select the most emotionally charged verbs and nouns for the bad thing you help them avoid. If you're helping customers do something good, select verbs and nouns that connote success.

Of all the options above, which tagline works the best?

Once you've come up with a good tagline, read it aloud several times. Can you say it in conversation without being self-conscious? If not, find the words you're getting hung up on and try substituting those out.

Test your tagline with friends who are not in your industry. Do they understand what you do? If not, ask them which part of the tagline is confusing and try to incorporate their thoughts to clarify.

When you have the right tagline, you'll know it.

TAGLINE DOS AND DON'TS

• Do collect other people's taglines and examine what works and what doesn't work. Apply what you notice about what works to your own tagline.

• Do devise a tagline that is unique to what you do and your way of doing it.

• Don't use flip, hip or esoteric taglines. They are often confusing, will eventually sound dated, and are rarely understandable to a wider (perhaps even international) audience.

• Don't make your tagline too general in the hopes of not alienating any prospects.

• Do ask strangers (and acquaintances) if they understand your business after seeing and hearing your tagline (and don't argue with them if they don't).

- Do keep it short. Sometimes you won't be able to fit everything into the tagline. Keep rephrasing and distilling until you have a pithy tagline that answers the questions: What do you do? For whom? What do they get?

- Do focus on the result of your work. People are looking for a solution, so start with that. Designers get caught up with how they do what they do—what tools they use, what process or methodology they've devised—but clients don't care about that. All they care about is the end result or benefit to them—or return on investment (ROI)—for example, more sales closed, cleaner design that generates more sales, lower customer acquisition costs or richer customer understanding.

PRESENTING YOURSELF AS A PROFESSIONAL

First impressions are important. Clients often decide whether they want to work with you based on the first impression you give. And that first impression is often based on the "package" you present, which includes your physical appearance (if they meet you in person first) or your virtual appearance (if they first meet you via e-mail or your web site). You must control that perception as much as possible by presenting a package that says, "I am a professional." This conveys an impression of confidence and professionalism that inspires trust in you and your abilities.

It goes without saying that the work you do must be of the highest quality. Beyond that, the professional package you present should include and integrate your business card, letterhead, web site, newsletter, brochures, and even tiny promotion tools (which often pack the strongest punch), such as the message on your voice mail and the details of your signature file.

We or I?

How you present yourself should balance the reality of who you are with the knowledge of what your clients need from you, or who they need you to be. This is another way of understanding the idea that everything flows from the market.

If you're a sole proprietor, referring to your company as "we" won't make you seem like a big corporation. It will, however, make you seem bigger than yourself. If that's important to your prospects, then it helps to get into the "we" habit.

If it doesn't matter to them or if being a sole proprietor makes them more comfortable with you—because it means they have easy access to you, for example—then, by all means, use "I" when referring to your company.

Some corporate clients will be more comfortable working with you if they see you have a network of resources available to serve their needs. Some clients will need to present their chosen resource to others in the company, and for that reason may need to perceive you as a larger entity. In this case, "we" is more appropriate, even if that "we" is simply you and your network of resources, or you and your dog.

However, more and more these days, prospects are working with solo practitioners and therefore know there are advantages to working with an independent. But no matter what size you are— one person working independently or with a network of alliances, a partnership, or a firm with a few employees—the important thing is to be upfront with your clients when you present yourself.

HOW TO TALK ABOUT YOUR SERVICES

The first objective of any marketing effort is to gain the opportunity to have a conversation with someone (prospect, referral source or potential unknown) about the work you do, and to find out what they may need.

Getting people to stop what they're doing to put their attention on you is easier said than done. That's why talking about your services is not actually about giving your pitch; it's more about sensing what the person is open to hearing at that moment, and then providing the right kind and amount of detail. In other words, you must be able to talk about your services, but in order to do that effectively, you must be able to read other people and respond accordingly.

So, how can you effectively answer the question "What do you do?"

It seems simple but, believe it or not, this is often one of the most difficult questions to answer. It becomes even more challenging when what you do is unique, specialized or new, or when you do a lot of different things. This section will provide several strategies for answering that question in a variety of situations and from a range of perspectives.

One of the reasons that question is difficult to answer is because you are probably not prepared and haven't given enough thought to the topic (or to self-promotion in general). In order to answer this question successfully, you must know what simple message you want to convey, then do so articulately and engagingly, and be able to do it in a variety of situations and varying time limits.

HAVING BLURBS FOR ALL SEASONS

In order to speak effectively and persuasively about your business, you need blurbs—that is, clear and concise words to describe what you do and who you do it for. A blurb is, in essence, your answer to the question, "What do you do?" And these blurbs need to be ready for action.

For example, you run into a colleague in an elevator. He asks you what you do, and you only have a few seconds to answer—which is why a blurb is often referred to as your "elevator speech." You need a simple sentence that piques your colleague's interest before he gets off on the eleventh floor. Your objective at that moment is to get him asking for more details—to stay on the elevator beyond his stop or to invite you to get off with him so you can keep talking.

Other times, you may have five long minutes to address a group, which may feel like an eternity because you can't imagine talking for that long about what you do. For those situations, you must know which details to elaborate on in order to convey the clearest picture of your talents and services without overwhelming listeners with too much information.

What you say also always depends on whom you're talking to. If it's a prospect who is familiar with your industry jargon, using it in your blurbs shows you know your stuff. If it's a neighbor, your jargon may be intimidating.

But we're getting ahead of ourselves. Let's start with the facts and benefits of your services and talents.

Your prospect has a need and what he wants to hear is how you can fulfill his need—"what's in it for me" (WIIFM). But if you don't know how to speak the language of WIIFM or benefits, he won't hear the points he needs to hear, which are the stepping stones from "I'm interested" to "You're hired."

Creating Your Blurbs

First, a warning: Don't ever answer the question "What do you do?" with a label, unless you are trying to stop the conversation. Don't say, "I'm a designer." Although it's short and sweet, it is actually one of the worst things you can say. Why?

First, labels leave too much room for interpretation. They mean different things to different people. If you say you're a "designer," and the person you're talking to thinks of an interior designer, you've already got a miscommunication. Also, the label you use is often industry jargon that you understand but may not be clear to your listener. Or they may hear your label and decide right then and there that they don't need "X" or aren't interested in "X."

Instead of labeling yourself, create a blurb that says what you do and who you do it for. For example, "I design annual reports for the healthcare and financial industries."

Do you see how that simple sentence includes what you do and who you do it for? This helps avoid miscommunication, and the listener could pick any of the words in that sentence and say, "Tell me more about that."

CREATE A BLURB

In this exercise, you will be creating different versions of your own blurb. Read through the directions first to get a sense of what you'll be thinking about, then go back and fill in the answers.

You might have ideas that don't fit into this format or structure, which is fine. Just use the exercise to stimulate your ideas. There is no right way to do this … you're simply opening up your mind.

What do you currently say when someone asks what you do?

Would the tagline you created make sense in answer to the question "What do you do?" If not, modify it so that it does.

Who are the clients you work with?

What problems do they experience?

Your 10-word blurb should answer the question "what do you do?" with three important pieces of information: what you do, who you do it for and what they get. Complete the formula below.

What you do:
For whom:
What they get:

Turn that info into your ten-word blurb.

Now write that blurb from a helping perspective.

I help (who?)_____

(do what?)_____

(so they can)_____.

Try that 10-word blurb from a problem-solving perspective.

I work with (whom?)_____

to solve (which problems?)_____

(which means they)_____.

Write a version that your mother (or any relative or kindly neighbor) would understand; make it as clear as possible since this person is genuinely interested but doesn't really understand your business, much less the specifics of what you do.

Write a version that would be understood by a stranger in the doctor's office or someone you meet at the dog park. This is the type of conversation that starts out as chitchat on the topic of whatever brought you together, but could easily turn toward work in those "you never know" type of situations—but only if your blurb is clear. (Also, for all of the questions that follow, imagine yourself talking to people who are positive and who would enjoy helping you, not someone who's going to judge or reject you.)

Write a version that would be understood by a colleague or business-person that you see on a regular basis (maybe at church or through a volunteer organization). This person doesn't know your industry but does understand business and has connections that could help you (only if they understand what you do).

Write a version that a colleague at a trade show or conference for your industry would understand. This person understands your jargon, so feel free to use it.

Now create your 25-word blurb, which will build on your ten-word blurb by adding specifics. (For example, "I help nonprofit organizations raise more money" becomes "I help nonprofit organizations raise more money by designing direct response letters and other marketing materials that make it really easy for people to give.")

Now write a 40-word blurb that continues to build on the 25-word blurb, but adds more details and drops a few names that your listener will recognize. (For example, "I help nonprofit organizations raise more money by designing direct response letters and other marketing materials that make it really easy for people to give" becomes "I help nonprofit organizations, such as the American Red Cross and The Humane Society, raise more money by designing direct response letters and other marketing materials that make it really easy for people to give.")

By this point, you should be well into the conversation and no longer relying on these blurbs.

Also, these blurbs don't need to be perfect, just good enough to work with so you can go out and test them on the real world. Then, talk to as many people as possible from all walks of life. You want to know if they understand. If not, ask them what they don't get and find the words to clarify. If their eyes start glazing over, your blurb needs work.

Tip: One way to be really clear about what you do is the "You know (blank), well I do (blank)" formula. For example, "You see the sign on top of that building? I make those."

DON'T SOUND LIKE A ROBOT

One danger of perfecting your blurbs, however, is that you may come off sounding like a robot. Or as if you're reciting lines that you've memorized because you can't remember what you do. Most blurbs have that quality to them.

So now that you know what to say, your challenge is to find a way to say it that is genuine, as if it's coming directly from you in the present moment (which it is) and as if it's the first time you've said it. So be sure to:

- Look directly into the person's eyes when you say it. That way, even if you've said it before, this is the first time you're saying it to her and looking at her reminds you of this.

- Let yourself be imperfect; that's what conversation is. And if you see that the person does not understand, stop and try again.

What if I Do More Than One Thing?

Most of us do more than just one thing. Some of us do many different things, even professionally. Maybe you offer two corollary services or specialize in two completely different markets. Which one should you mention first? Or maybe the things you do have nothing to do with each other. How will you know which one to say, or which one to say first? How do you know whether saying the wrong one will put the listener off and not stick around to hear about the other one, even if that's exactly what he or she needs at that moment?

Here are a few different ways to deal with the myriad situations that come up if you are in this boat:

- Apply the 80/20 rule (also called the Pareto principle, after its founder, the Italian economist Vilfredo Pareto, who first wrote about it in 1895). The rule says that 20 percent of your activities will account for 80 percent of your results. So: 20 percent of your customers will account for 80 percent of your sales, 20 percent of your services will account for 80 percent of your profits, and so on. So if you know which "thing you do" accounts for 80 percent of your income, say that one first.

- Focus on two main things. It's hard for people to hold more than a couple things at a time in their minds, so if you can't (or don't want to) choose between the two things you do, use your shortest blurbs for each and then preface what you say with, "I do two main things: First, I teach people how to promote their services, and second, I tutor young children in reading in a community center." Then be quiet and let your listener choose which one to ask about. Or, at the end, you can say, "Which one would you like to hear about?" or "Which is of more interest to you?"

- Flip a coin and let chance be your guide. It could take the conversation in a completely unexpected direction, which isn't a bad thing.

BE THE FIRST TO ASK

In an effort to avoid wasting time telling people what they don't need to know, you must quickly figure out what they may be open to or looking for, so that you can respond directly to that need. But you can't read minds, so how will you know?

Here's a trick: Don't wait for them to ask what you do; you ask first what they do. Be in research mode, especially when meeting new people. Be fishing for details that will help you hone your own presentation, telling you what to focus on for their purposes.

MARKETING SYNTAX: THE LANGUAGE OF RESULTS

Robert Middleton, of Action Plan Marketing, has devised a concept to help you attract more clients and talk about what you do in a way that engages them in a conversation. It's called Marketing Syntax, which he calls the language of results.

Syntax is the order of the words you use to form phrases and sentences. Marketing Syntax is the order in which marketing messages are arranged to generate attention, interest, desire and action. If you use the right order, you get better results than if you use the wrong order.

The most effective messages are usually arranged in this order: Target Market—Problem—Outcome—Value—Proof—Offer. Here's a brief summary of how it works for networking scenarios.

- **Target Market**. Start here because people want to know that you recognize and understand them. You let them know immediately that your message is for them. *"I work with..."*

- **Problem**. Next, talk about the problems, challenges, issues and predicaments they are facing. This shows that you understand them and can relate to them. They automatically want to know how you can help. *"... who have XYZ challenges..."*

- **Outcome**. The next thing people want to know is what ultimate outcome or solution they'll get from you. They want to be assured you can actually help. *"Our clients say the main thing they get from us is..."*

- **Value**. Next, people want to know more about the various benefits they can expect to receive. So all the benefits you provide is very welcome news. *"And some of the key benefits they receive are..."*

- **Proof**. Then they want some proof that you've done this kind of work before with people like them. And the best way to give proof is by telling success stories. *"A client we worked with recently had a similar issue…"*

- **Offer.** Finally, after you've gotten this far, you need to offer something. People at this point want even more information about your ideas. *"I have an article that explains this in more detail. Can I send it to you?"*

MARKETING SYNTAX IN PRACTICE

Now here's your chance to put those ideas into practice.

Target Market. With whom do you work? (Example: I work with creative people …)

> I work with:

Problem. What problems, challenges, issues and predicaments are they facing? (Example: … who hate to market themselves.)

> … who:

Outcome. What ultimate outcome or solution will they get from working with you? (Example: My clients tell me the main thing they learn is how to be persistent in their marketing efforts.)

> My clients say the main thing they get from me is:

Value. What other benefits can they expect to receive? (Example: They also learn how to see every encounter as a potential marketing opportunity, and many of them have even started to enjoy their self-promotion.)

> And some of the key benefits they receive are:

Proof. What are some success stories that demonstrate those benefits? (Example: A recent client just couldn't make time for her marketing unless she had someone to be accountable to. The Marketing Mentor program gave her the structure she needed to fit it into her day and her life. She either had to do her marketing or confess to me that she hadn't—and that was enough motivation for her to get it done. Eventually, she was able to do it for herself.)

> "A client we worked with recently had a similar issue ... "

Offer. Make an offer of more information about your ideas. (Example: Would you like to receive my free e-mail newsletter with marketing tips every two weeks?)

> Would you be interested in ...

ENGAGE YOUR LISTENERS WITH STORIES

One of the reasons you may have trouble talking about your work is because you imagine it will come across as bragging. And your mother taught you not to brag, right?

If you say, "I'm the best designer on the planet," that, indeed, would be bragging. But you can talk about the work that you do and the effect it has without bragging. That's merely stating the facts.

First, though, you must make a distinction between yourself and your work. Then simply focus on the work. It may help to avoid using the word "I." Instead, start your sentences with "my clients" or "my projects," then focus on what you do and the results it generates. Use verbs rather than adjectives. (Leave the adjectives to your clients in the form of testimonials, or to the press in the form of publicity. They can say you're "the best" and it won't be bragging at all.)

One novel way to convey this information is by telling stories about what you do and what you have done. When someone asks about the work you do, instead of listing your accomplishments or reciting your résumé, tell them a story.

Everyone loves a good story. It's ideal for a sit-down networking luncheon or on a plane, situations where you can say more than your blurbs, where you have a little more time to chat. People relax to listen, bringing one level of defense down. Also, stories inspire, motivate and engage people. We tend to listen closely to stories told with genuine enthusiasm and passion, no matter what the story's about. Your listeners may immediately start identifying with characters in your story, thinking to themselves, "Oh yeah, that happened to me, too," or "I need someone to help me with that, too." It won't be long before they're asking for your card.

Tell stories about projects you've worked on, with emphasis on the outcome that resulted from the effort you put in—how you were a hero and saved the day. Use examples that your listeners will relate to and that reinforce the focus you want them to see. Include characters they can identify with, a situation that would be familiar to them or a crisis that might be just like the one they're in right now.

FOUR ELEMENTS EVERY STORY MUST HAVE

1. A strong, passionate voice. Good stories that draw people in require a storyteller who conveys passion for the business. And even if you're the shy type, remember that your story is not about you, it's about your work.

2. Evidence of your specialty in your listeners' industries. You want your prospects to see themselves in the characters in the stories you tell. You'll know when they do because they'll be nodding their heads, knowing that you understand their needs and that you can help them.

3. A climax. There should be a moment of suspense in your story and everything should build up to it. If the project involved research, the presentation of the data could figure as the moment of suspense. Be creative. Embellish for effect.

4. Drama and romance. Romance is not just boy meets girl. Romance is adventure. Romance is life—someone else's. You can plant little seeds of drama and romance in your story, elements that make people wonder what happened, without giving them all the details. This will keep them interested.

MINING YOUR OWN STORIES

You don't have to be a writer to tell stories about your work. All you need is a little imagination. This exercise will help you develop stories that you can use at a moment's notice to engage your listener or reader. Use them in conversation or in writing. Include them in your brochure, in your e-mail marketing campaign and on your web site in a section entitled "Success Stories."

Tell the story of one of the top three projects you've worked on. Telling this story is like promoting the kind of work you want the most, which could help bring more projects just like it to you.

Situation/Plot (the problem that was presented to you)
Characters (include a description of your client)
Climax (include how you solved the problem, and the results)
Story

Tell the story of the project you're currently working on. This will be freshest in your mind and come across with the most details, since they are right on the tip of your tongue.

Situation/Plot (the problem that was presented to you)
Characters (include a description of your client)
Climax (include how you solved the problem, and the results)
Story

Tell the story of a project that wasn't going so well, in which an unexpected problem arose but you took action and saved the day. This shows the whole picture and acknowledges the reality that things don't always go smoothly, which makes listeners trust you even more.

Situation/Plot (the problem that was presented to you)

Characters (include a description of your client)
Climax (include how you solved the problem, and the results)
Story

WHAT ARE YOUR FACTS AND BENEFITS?

Have you ever thought about the facts and benefits of working with you? Aside from the impressions people have about what you do, there are objective, concrete facts that can set you apart from the competition. But facts alone are not enough. The benefits of your facts will tell your listener "what's in it for me"—WIIFM.

Facts are concrete, and they include things like your geographical location, your area of expertise and your professional background. Benefits are subjective and may be different for each prospect, depending on his or her needs. Benefits illustrate to a prospect why she needs you and how you will help her. The benefits you show her will compel her to work with you instead of with someone else.

First, let's find your facts. They are so elemental to your work that they may be hard to identify at first. You can find facts about your work by asking yourself some simple questions. For example, how long have you been doing this work? If the answer is "twenty years," that fact in itself is not relevant to your prospect. But the benefit of that fact is. To find the benefit of this fact, put yourself in your prospect's shoes to ask the (slightly rude) question "So what? How will your twenty years in business help me?"

Each fact has at least one benefit, and often more. Here are a few of the benefit statements created from the fact "I have been a designer for twenty years."

- My valuable experience will save you time and money.
- I know what works and what doesn't.
- I am familiar with your needs, your competition and your market.
- I have a track record doing this work.

Make sense? See how many different ways there are of saying why this fact will help your client?

Now it's your turn.

FACTS AND BENEFITS IN PRACTICE

Talking about your work is rarely easy. But if you use this exercise to turn your facts into benefits, most of the work will be done. Then, as you listen to your prospect's needs, you can tailor your response to her, pointing out only the benefits most relevant to her situation.

List five benefits for each of the facts below.

1. Where are you located?

Fact:

Benefits:

   1.

   2.

   3.

   4.

   5.

2. What services do you offer?

Fact:

Benefits:

   1.

   2.

   3.

   4.

   5.

3. What is your specialty? (There may be more than one.)

Fact:

Benefits:

1.

2.

3.

4.

5.

4. What skills and talents do you have?

Fact:

Benefits:

1.

2.

3.

4.

5.

5. What was your last project?

Fact:

Benefits:

1.

2.

3.

4.

5.

6. What clients have you worked with in the past?

Fact:

Benefits:

1.

2.

3.

4.

5.

7. What industries have you worked in?

Fact:

Benefits:

1.

2.

3.

4.

5.

8. What resources do you have available to you?

Fact:

Benefits:

1.

2.

3.

4.

5.

Now you have a foundation of information to use to present your-self and your services—your business name, your domain name, a tagline, more blurbs than you'll ever need and all the facts and benefits about your business.

Enough about you. Let's move on to the marketing tools and tricks you'll use to reach your prospects.

CHAPTER 4
WHICH MARKETING TOOLS SHOULD I USE?

When it comes to choosing which marketing tools to use, many designers are overwhelmed. It's hard to know which ones are most effective and will give you the most bang for your buck.

This chapter will cover the five essential marketing tools that are most effective and least expensive and that, when used to support each other, will bring you into contact with your ideal clients:

1. **Networking.** Attend at least two events per month to keep meeting new prospects and filling the pipeline.
2. **E-mail marketing.** Send a monthly message to keep your visibility high.
3. **Online presence.** Have that essential online presence, whether with a web site, blog or portfolio site.
4. **Cold calling.** Take charge of your marketing and reach out to the companies you really want to work with.
5. **Promotional piece.** Have something tangible to send the prospects who want to know more.

There are other marketing tools, of course, and you may want to integrate these five with others. But do so thoughtfully.

When you choose which marketing opportunities to spend your time and money on, there are two questions you should always keep in mind:

1. Is it related to your target market(s)?
2. Does this tool get you to your goal (such as garnering five new clients in a certain market by second quarter)?

If the answer is no to either or both of these questions, it's not usually a good use of resources. This is especially important when you have limited time (or money) to spend on marketing.

Don't just do something because it's easy or cheap. For example, don't buy a mailing list just because the salesman keeps calling; only buy it if you are certain that the list will get you to your target market.

NETWORKING

Meeting your prospects in person is, hands down, one of the best ways to make a strong impression, find out what they need and get their contact information. Yet, so many designers don't want to leave the studio, much less find the places where their prospects gather.

That was the case for Peter Levinson of LevinsonBlock in New York City, a small firm specializing in nonprofits since 1981. Word of mouth had brought most projects to the firm. But Peter recently had a slow year, and he knew he needed to find more nonprofits if he wanted to keep his doors open.

Although he dreaded the idea of networking, he did some online research, found the New York chapter of a group called the

Association of Fundraising Professionals (AFP) and went to his first monthly meeting.

There were forty people at the event and, to Peter's surprise, everyone he met was friendly. He talked to ten people, though none had a burning need for his design services, and collected five cards. His review of the first meeting: "It wasn't a nightmare."

At the second monthly AFP meeting, four of the people he met qualified as prospects—they needed design services. He continued to attend meetings as well as the annual conference, and he has made some good connections, had some opportunities come his way and even garnered some business.

Networking Tools

Networking tools are, by nature, very small and very powerful. Those tools alone—your business card, e-mail address, signature file, nametags and more—could be enough to build your business, but only if you pay close attention and use them with marketing in mind.

Your Business Card

Your business card is just a tiny piece of paper, but its value is disproportionate to its size. Because space is limited, the weight of each word on your card is exponentially greater than it would be if it were buried in the middle of a brochure or letter. So be sure to give it careful consideration before you spend a lot of money on beautiful four-color cards with your new logo and tagline. Don't rush into printing your business cards, which many people do because suddenly they have an event to attend and they have no cards to take.

Instead, simply design a temporary card using an online resource, such as www.iprint.com or www.vistaprint.com. Don't agonize over what goes on the temporary card. As long as it has your contact information, you can pass it out and you will look more professional than if you have none at all.

As a designer, you will, of course, design a card that looks great. But the question to ask yourself is whether it "works" from a marketing point of view. It will, if you follow these business card dos and don'ts:

- Do make it look professional. There are no rules about what a business card should look like; just make sure it looks as professional as the market you intend to attract. Look closely at the cards of colleagues and competitors. In fact, you should have a collection of business cards, and you should always be analyzing the cards that you collect to see what works for you—beyond design—from a marketing point of view.

- Do have more than one card. There's no rule that says you have to fit everything on a single card. If you have a couple different specialties, why not have a card for each? That will make you look even more perfect to the prospect whose need is reflected even more specifically on your card.

- Do make it interesting, so people will take a close look at it. It can be undersized, oversized or interestingly sized, colorful or printed on an unusual paper stock. All of these aspects will make someone stop and take a look (and maybe even comment) when you hand it to them, and will be part of the initial impression they take from their encounter with you.

Don't worry if your card is not the standard size; a few people may complain, but they'll remember you.

- Do use both sides. When you walk away from an encounter, your business card stays and represents you, so make sure it has all the essential information on it. Don't hesitate to use the back as well. It can be a place for people to make notes (in which case, adding the word "Notes" encourages people to write a note about you or your meeting with them). Or it can be a place to list the various services you offer, so that when you walk away and the prospects suddenly wonder, "Hmm, I wonder if she designs web sites," that next level of detail on your card will help them answer the question.

- Don't clutter up the card. You have a very small space to work with, so clarity is essential. You need to include your all of your basic contact information, but that isn't so simple anymore, when everyone has a name, a company name, a tagline, an address, a landline phone number, a cell phone number, a fax number, an e-mail address, a web address, etc.

- Don't get creative with placement of this information. Think instead about what makes the most sense to the person looking at the card. For example, put your tagline under or close to your company name, not floating somewhere in the middle of the card just because it looks cool.

EIGHT WAYS TO MAKE THE MOST
OF YOUR BUSINESS CARD

If networking is the most effective marketing activity—and it is—
then your business card is your networking ticket. It's essential, yet
disposable. Its purpose is to create a first impression, over and over,
to be there at the right moment, not to be kept as an heirloom. Here
are a few ways to use your business card most effectively:

1. Don't leave home without it. Carry a few everywhere you go.
   Even if you're walking the dog or going to the gym and you can't
   imagine running into anyone who'll want it, bring a few cards.
   Store a few in your locker at the gym.

2. Keep them in every pocket or handbag. Stash a few in every
   purse, briefcase and piece of luggage you own. That way, you
   won't have to remember so often to replenish the one container
   where you keep them. Keep a stack in your car and near the
   doors of your home and office. Put them by your keys or wherever you'll look before going out. Put a few in your wallet, especially for those unexpected marketing moments when you meet
   someone standing in line at the bank or post office. Get in the
   habit of asking yourself, "Do I have my business cards on me?"

3. Bring more than you think you need. You can't represent yourself
   if you don't have enough cards to give to the contacts that you
   make, so don't underestimate how many you'll need.

4. Hand them to people when you shake hands. They'll remember
   your name better if they see it in writing. Develop the reflex of

handing over your card, and don't be shy if they don't automatically reciprocate. Go ahead and ask for their cards. It will help you remember their names, an invaluable marketing skill in itself. Offer one to everyone you are introduced to or with whom you start a conversation. Get in the habit of saying, "Let me give you my card."

5. Give them to people every time you meet them, not just the first time. This will avoid any embarrassment in case they forget your name. It doesn't matter if they don't keep the card; it will have already served its purpose.

6. Include one in everything you send out, including introductory letters, invoices, FYIs and article tear sheets.

7. Ask for two cards from the people you meet. Tell them you want one for yourself and one you can pass along to anyone you come into contact with who might need their services. This sets you up perfectly to give two cards for the same purpose. It couldn't hurt.

8. Make notes on cards when you get them from people you meet. Put the date and event on each card, along with a note that will help you remember the person. Do it while the person is standing there. This helps to create trust.

Your E-Mail Address

Don't underestimate the power of your e-mail address. Besides networking, your e-mail is one of your most important marketing tools, and it can either work for you or against you. This is one of those little things that make a huge impact and has a tremendous amount of power for the amount of time most people spend thinking about it.

Why? Because, like your name or your company name, it is often the only thing a prospect or client will see, whether in the "from" field of an e-mail message you've sent, in a list of e-mail addresses or in your post on a blog or forum. If your e-mail address clearly says what you do, someone seeing it who is in need of your services could make the connection and reach out to find out more.

But if your e-mail address doesn't convey any meaning about what you do or who you do it for, then you may be missing as many marketing opportunities as e-mail messages you send out.

Plus, many people don't read (or even open) e-mail messages from people they don't know. If they recognize it, they open it; if they don't recognize it, they delete it with a single click. (Maybe you do this, too.)

Ideally, your e-mail address should include your domain name, even if you haven't launched your web site yet (and you should have, by the way). That way, everyone who sees it knows automatically that there is a web site to visit if they want more information. If your e-mail address doesn't include your domain name, people will assume you don't have one, and that reflects negatively on your professionalism.

Let's look at some examples:

- We can't tell anything from DMRSBTG@isp.com—not who it is, whether it's a man or woman, or what kind of work he or she does.

- What about fdoubleo7@isp.com? F, for Frank, is the person's name, and 007 is James Bond, who may be Frank's hero. This is way too personal for a professional e-mail address. If you must use something like this for yourself, just make sure you have another one for professional situations.

- headsetladies@isp.com is the e-mail address of a woman whose company sells (or makes, that's not quite clear) headsets. The use of the word "ladies" adds some personality in a way that headsets@ or headsetcompany@ wouldn't.

- Your best e-mail address is: yourname@yourdomainname.com.

Your Sig File

Your *sig file* (short for signature file) is one of the simplest Internet marketing tools there is. It's also one of the most effective, because it is unobtrusive and well-accepted by most everyone online.

Your sig file is a block of text with your contact information (often with a link and sometimes an image) that is added to every e-mail message you send out. It not only lets you identify who you are, what you do and where you are located, it also can make it supremely easy for prospects to get in touch with you in the way that's most comfortable for them.

Your e-mail software should have a way for you to create your sig file that either gets automatically attached to each message or that you can attach yourself each time.

Having a sig file is important because when your prospects are in their moment of need for your services or products, they not only need to remember you, they also need to be able to find your contact information without wasting too much time. It's important to add your sig file to every message you send because you don't know when someone will want to pick up the phone. And it's not likely they'll go looking through every message you've ever sent to find your phone number or web address.

What should be in your sig file?

You sig file should include all the possible ways for someone to reach you, plus a link to your web site. Your sig file should have your complete contact information—office phone, cell phone, fax number, toll-free number, e-mail address, mailing address, web site, even your office hours.

What can be in your sig file?

You can get creative with your sig file by including images, logos, testimonials and other interesting quotations. For ideas, take a look at the sig files in the messages in your inbox.

Here is one example:

Ilise Benun
Marketing Mentor
(201) 653-0783
Ilise@marketing-mentor.com
http://www.marketing-mentor.com

Sign up for Quick Tips from Marketing Mentor here:
http://www.marketing-mentortips.com/

And here's another example:

Steven Morris
Morris! Communication | strategic cross-media branding

950 Sixth Avenue, Ste. 212, San Diego, CA 92101

(: 619 234 1211 x111

8: steven@thinkmorris.com

www.thinkmorris.com

Your Voice Mail Message

Don't miss marketing opportunities while you're out attending a networking luncheon or meeting with clients. Your outgoing phone message is another first-impression maker that can do double duty as a valuable marketing tool.

If your prospects are calling you, they probably already know something about what you do, so your message doesn't need to be a sales pitch. But do make it professional, friendly, informative and succinct. Provide general information about your services, but also give callers a way to skip past it if they just want to leave a message.

Your voice mail message should include any information necessary to take the next step toward working with you, such as:

- A concise blurb about the services you offer

- All the different ways to contact you (e.g., address, fax, e-mail)— just like your sig file

- Your schedule (If you start early in the morning, let people know that. If you take Fridays off, let them know that as well. It also doesn't hurt to give them the best time to reach you.)

- Your web address, so that if people want to do a little research while they're waiting for you to return the call, they can

Change your voice mail message regularly to keep it fresh; every week is good, but every day is even better. Make it part of your morning routine.

Thank-You Notes

The most personal marketing tool also has the strongest impact. Yes, you can say thank you via e-mail, but it means so much more if you do it on real paper. Why? Because most everybody's mail these days is nothing but junk and bills. A personal note, with a handwritten address and a funky stamp, stands out in that pile. It sparkles and shimmers, like a mirage in the desert. "Could it really be," the recipient is thinking, "something actually for me?"

They open it and find a lovely and thoughtful note from you, handwritten on elegant stationery, that refers to something that passed between you. This is a rare jewel in today's mailbox, and it is interpreted as "Wow, this person cares" or "This person is real" or "This person actually took the time to do this for me." Needless to say, this is a good impression to convey.

Don't be shy in expressing your gratitude. You can use these personal notes to thank a prospect for meeting with you, to thank a colleague for making a referral (regardless of whether anything actually comes of the referral), for a gift or a thought or an idea—anything. But do it sooner rather than later.

All you need is a box of cards, or even a stack of postcards, with examples of your work. Put them by your desk with a book of stamps within reaching distance, because if you have to get up, you won't do it.

The only remaining challenge will be to make sure you have the physical address of your recipients. Make it your duty to collect business cards for this purpose. You can always e-mail the person and simply ask for his or her address. So don't let that tiny task prevent you from making this high-impact and impressive impression.

This will really set you apart, plus it takes you a couple steps along the road of developing that personal relationship so key to doing business. A personal note really shows you took extra time to get in touch. People will notice.

USE YOUR MEMORY AS A MARKETING TOOL

Do you insist that you can't remember names?

Remembering the name of someone you meet is important because it shows you care enough to pay attention.

Remembering is all about listening. In fact, if you listen, you don't have to remember. You just will. Here are a few techniques to try the next time you meet someone new:

- Repeat the person's name, then use it in your response to them.
- Visualize the name by writing it down, or simply ask for the person's card (and be sure to look at the name until it registers).
- Create an association to their name in your mind. (This, however, is not my favorite technique because it takes you away from listening and you may miss something crucial.)

When meeting someone again, it's also important to remember what you discussed last time you talked, what they were working on, and especially what they were struggling with. All of this makes a strong impact—an impact that says, "I cared enough to pay attention."

E-MAIL MARKETING

Introduce Yourself to New Prospects via E-Mail

There is nothing wrong with using e-mail to introduce yourself and your services to someone who's never heard of you before, as long as you have something of value to offer. If done selectively and personally, e-mail can be an extremely effective way to initiate a relationship with a company you really want to work with.

Start with an introductory phone call. If you don't get through, leave a message with your name, the reason for your call ("I'm calling to find out whether you work with design firms") and your web site address, where they can see samples. Then tell them you'll also send an e-mail message. (You can usually get the e-mail address by telling the receptionist that you've been playing phone tag with so and so and would like to send an e-mail message.)

Follow up with an e-mail. In your e-mail message, refer to your voice mail message and repeat your request. Offer something you know will be of value, such as a sample of work you did for a company just like theirs. They may be very tempted to respond to you.

Here's an example of an e-mail message you can tailor for your own purposes:

> *Bob, on the heels of my voice mail message, I'm wondering if you would like to see samples of collateral materials for software companies. If so, just reply to this message with your mailing address, and I'll send them along. Some of our clients are (drop names here), and you can see the samples here as well: (link to that page on your web site).*

Some people are more comfortable responding to an e-mail message than picking up the phone and returning a phone call, partially because they can do it at their own convenience, outside of business hours if necessary. By using e-mail in conjunction with the phone, you increase the odds that you will get a response.

Send Regular E-Mail Messages to Your In-House List

An e-mail marketing campaign—sending regular e-mail messages to everyone you know and everyone who knows you—is a great way to market your services because it can consistently accomplish many things at once. It can showcase your creativity, increase your visibility and build credibility, while also distinguishing you from the competition. Plus, it's the best way to drive traffic to your web site because it's much more reliable and targeted than the search engines.

What prevents many designers from creating their own e-mail campaign is the time required to create the content each time. But it doesn't have to be overwhelming. Once you find a template and a formula that works, all you have to do is treat your campaign like a client project and devote the necessary time to it.

Here are some ideas for content:

- Provide case studies and real-life examples. People love to see what others like them have done, which means they will take time to read a simple case study that describes a problem you solved for a client. This is a good springboard to offer more general advice. Showing how you've helped clients address specific challenges is good from a promotional perspective, too, because it gives concrete examples of the work you do, which can otherwise seem abstract to those who hire you.

- Offer a list of your top three to five tips on a subject. There must be hints you can give your clients and prospects about how to make the process of working with you go smoothly. Turn these hints into tips, like "How to hire a designer" or "How to get great work from a designer."

- Answer your clients' frequently asked questions. Keep track of the questions your clients ask, whether via e-mail or in person. Then answer each one in a short article. If you can't think of any questions, send your current clients a quick message asking for their questions.

- Offer your opinion on a hot topic. Don't be afraid to tackle the hot issues in your field. Offer your own expert opinion—your readers want to know.

You also don't have to create all the content from scratch. You can simply pass along links to articles, web sites and blogs that would be of interest or useful to your market.

E-mail keeps you visible, keeps your market connected to you and motivates people to respond. Most important, it is the back and forth nature of e-mail that builds relationships. If you do your e-mail marketing right, your recipients will actually look forward to receiving your messages. They may even thank you. (More about this in Chapter Six.)

ONLINE PRESENCE

If you want to be taken seriously as a professional, you really must have a presence in cyberspace. Ideally, that would be your own web site at www.yourname.com or www.yourcompanyname.com.

But if you're not ready to put the time and money into developing that full-fledged site, you do have other options.

The first is to create your own simple site using free, open source software, which is offered at sites such as www.joomla.org and http://drupal.org. These are both content management systems (CMS) that will help you build anything from a simple one-page site to a complex corporate web site.

Portfolio Sites

Another option is to post samples of your work on one (or more) digital portfolio sites, such as www.creativehotlist.com and www.portfolios.com, or on the sites of trade associations, such as the Graphic Artists Guild, www.gag.org, where web space for a portfolio is offered as a member benefit.

You can use a digital portfolio site as a "portal" to your own web site (which is ideal) or as your one-and-only online portfolio. If you choose the latter, there will be limitations on how much work you can show and how you show it, due to the structure they provide. On your own web site, though, you are free to organize and display the work in whatever way you think works best.

So how do you decide what to do? If possible, you should have both a web site and your work posted on digital portfolio sites. But the important question to keep in mind when deciding is this: Where do your prospects go when they need to find a designer? Whether they will look offline or online depends on what they're used to and what is convenient at the moment.

They may go to "the books," those familiar but oh-so-heavy directories of creative resources, or they may go to their own personal address books. The organized ones may check the paper files where they've been stuffing promotional materials for years. The busy ones may simply ruffle through their most recent pile of mail. The resourceful ones might pick up the phone to call someone who knows a lot of people. But most will go online.

They may begin their search online with the familiar, but perhaps not most effective, search engines, such as Google or Yahoo. Or they may start offline then go online to look for more samples on a web site. The reality is that they probably will use a combination of search tools, online and offline, to get the help they need. That's why it makes sense to have both a web site and your digital portfolio posted in a couple different places in cyberspace.

When it comes to searching, fewer options can be a blessing. In fact, one of the reasons buyers go to the portfolio sites is because there is already a filter in place to screen out the irrelevant (and overwhelming) results that are usually accessed through the major search engines.

So one advantage of posting your digital portfolio on portfolio sites is that these sites can drive prospects directly to you, including buyers who probably wouldn't otherwise find you—which can only add to your own self-promotion efforts.

POPULAR DIGITAL PORTFOLIO SITES

- Creative Hotlist
  www.creativehotlist.com

- theispot.com
  www.theispot.com

- Graphic Artists Guild
  www.gag.org

- Workbook
  www.workbook.com

- PlanetPoint
  www.planetpoint.com

- The Black Book
  www.blackbook.com

- Folioplanet
  http://folioplanet.com

- The Alternative Pick
  http://altpick.com

- Portfolios.com
  www.portfolios.com

Web Sites and Blogs

Not only do you need an online presence, but that presence must make it easy for your prospects to see your work and clearly see that you can help them.

A web site can be one of the most effective marketing tools you will ever use because it can help you expand your business in ways never before possible. It shows that you're up-to-date, gives you instant credibility and expands your market globally.

Most important, the World Wide Web provides anytime access to examples of your work. Your prospects can get information when they need it, without having to wait for you to send it, making it supremely simple for anyone to check you out and satisfy the desire for instant gratification that is pervasive in our digital economy.

But many designer sites convey a different message. Many say, "This is the web site of an artist." They are gorgeous to look at but impossible to navigate. They put image before purpose and don't address the clients' needs at all.

If you want your web site to be an effective marketing tool, it must be designed with the needs of your clients and prospects in the forefront of your mind, and it must convey the message "This is the web site of creative professionals who can help you solve your business problems."

What Your Web Site Can Do for You

First your web site shows that yours is a legitimate business, while at the same time giving a taste of your work—though there is no need to show everything. Use your web site to highlight the kind of work you want by showing those samples (and not showing the work you don't want more of). Providing a way for visitors to give you their contact information (in exchange for your e-mail newsletter, for example) can help you build a mailing list for future marketing efforts. And finally, a web site can help you weed out "bad" prospects who may not want to fill out a "request for estimate" form you have posted on the site.

What Your Web Site Can't Do for You

There is a lot of "build it and they will come" hype about web sites, but it's simply not true. You may build it, but then it's one of billions out there, with millions of sites added every day. Talk about information overload! That's why it's your responsibility to drive traffic to your site.

People talk about "getting work from their web site." That doesn't make sense. You can get work "through" your web site, but not from the site. The work comes from clients. So keep your expectations realistic for your web site; if you do, you'll be very satisfied with its performance.

The Essential Pages of your Web Site

Homepage. This is the most important page on your site. It's where your prospects will decide whether to go any further, so you must do everything you can on the homepage to lead them further into the site. Make sure your homepage isn't cluttered. And don't do the "We are a graphic design firm that … blah, blah, blah." There's nothing more boring or uninviting. Plus, it leaves out the most important piece of information: how your business can help the visitors.

It may seem strange, but don't focus your homepage on you and your services. This is not the place. It's more appropriate to do that one level deeper into the site. On the homepage, focus instead on the visitors' problems.

Notice the predominance of the word "you" in this homepage text for Colleen Wainwright at www.communicatrix-designs.com.

About us. This is where you tell your visitors a little about you. Include your credentials, your background, even photos of you and your staff. This is an especially important trust-building section of the site. Because the web is so anonymous, the more you can convey about the people behind the site, the better.

Here's another site (www.brand-x.us) that focuses on what the visitors may be experiencing—in this case, embarrassment—then offers the services of this company as a solution to the problem.

Services. Be sure to outline clearly the various services you offer, and do so in language that your prospects and visitors will be using. You want the language on your site to mirror the language already in their minds, another example of how everything flows from the market. It could be the subtle difference between using the word "samples" (which is what they're probably looking for) instead of the word "work" (which may be how you think of your samples).

Client list. This is one of the first things prospects look for on your web site. Not only do they want to see who you've worked with, they especially want to know whether you have experience working with others like them. Your goal is to position your services within certain markets and to demonstrate your expertise; your client list should be organized to achieve that goal. Instead of a static alphabetical list of company names, order them by industry served, medium, or both, if possible.

Your client list also should link to actual samples of work you've done for those clients or to testimonials from them. Don't worry if every name doesn't have a link. And don't worry about revealing your client list to your competitors. It's more important for your prospects to know who you're working with than for your competition not to know.

Portfolio. This is the most obvious reason to have a web site: to provide that anytime access to examples of your work. But don't show everything. The purpose of the site is to give your prospects a taste of your work, your style and your qualifications. Your portfolio should highlight the best of your work, with an emphasis on the type of work you want to do more of. If, for example, you have lots of small display ads but you don't want to do those anymore, don't include them in your portfolio.

Testimonials. You might be surprised at the power of testimonials (what other people say about working with you). Especially in such an anonymous medium as the web, anything real or genuine can have a very powerful effect. Include a page of testimonials from your clients, or sprinkle them throughout the site. The best place is in your portfolio section, with the actual work being shown.

Links page. Your web site should be a resource to your market, and one way to make it so is to provide links to other sites with information they would find useful. This also will help your search engine rankings because other sites will start linking to yours, and it's those links that make your site "popular" in the eyes of Google and other search engines.

Contact form. This is the place your prospects and visitors can tell you they've visited. If you don't have a contact form or a way to capture their contact information, you will never know who visited and, worse yet, you won't be able to stay in touch with them.

Contact information. More and more, people are using the web instead of the phone book when they want to find someone's contact information. So make sure yours is easy to find on your site. Ideally, you should put it on every page, but especially make sure it is on your homepage.

MAKING YOUR SITE USER-FRIENDLY

Is your site intuitive?

- Does it behave consistently throughout?
- How clear is it how to use the site?

Is your site visually consistent?

- Does it follow conventions that your users are familiar with?
- Is it obvious from one page to another that you're on the same site?
- How quickly can first-time visitors find what they're looking for?

Is your site efficient?

- Does it download fast enough for your users?
- Does it take less than three clicks for users to find the content they're looking for?
- Does the site reflect a clear understanding of your users and their needs?

Is your site supportive?

- Does it provide guidance and instruction when it's not obvious what to do?

Is your site engaging?

- Do users feel in control?
- Do users enjoy their experiences?

Adapted from from *Designing Websites:// for Every Audience* by Ilise Benun (HOW Design Books, 2003)

Blogs for Designers

Should you have a blog? That's a popular question these days.

The answer: It depends.

If you don't yet have a web site, a blog is one simple way to have one. A blog takes ten minutes to create, and you don't need any technical expertise. However, as with the portfolio sites, you have less freedom with the layout due to the limitations of most blog publishing software, especially the free ones (like www.blogger.com).

If you already have a web site and are trying to decide between an e-mail newsletter and a blog, note the main difference: a blog is a "pull" (i.e., readers have to find it and go there) while an e-mail marketing newsletter is a "push" (i.e., you send it to those you want to keep in touch with). Actually, these two tools—a blog and an e-mail newsletter—can work beautifully together. You can drive traffic to your blog by including links to it in your e-mail messages. And you can bulk up your newsletter subscriber list by linking to it and talking about it on your blog.

Colleen Wainwright, aka "the communicatrix" and a designer who blogs, says, "Blogs are conversations, not ads. Blogs are less promotional and less formal than a traditional static web site, so you can speak in your 'everyday' voice, which is often more friendly and approachable. Also, you can combine personal and professional elements in your blog; how much depends on what you're comfortable with, and what your prospective clientele will be comfortable reading about you."

Blogging also is improved by visuals, so designers are perfectly positioned to show their style. A small description, a bit of information or counterpoint to the image, and you're finished. That's the strategy behind Tina Roth Eisenberg's blog, www.swissmiss.com. Tina posts an eclectic collection of links and images that demonstrates her personal aesthetic in all sorts of design, including industrial design, furniture, graphic design and more. She also doesn't hesitate to write personal posts about her life, about things that make her smile and about other interesting discoveries she makes.

Tina posts every day, sometimes several times a day, spending about an hour each day adding to her blog. Her blog gets an impressive 150,000–200,000 visitors per month. "People seem to appreciate the variety I offer," Tina says. "My blog posts clearly showcase my aesthetics and prove that I am out there, trying to be on top of what's going on in the design and online world. Maybe visitors sense that and appreciate the honesty and personal touch behind it."

But is a blog an effective marketing tool?

It can be, but it's indirect. You shouldn't expect to "get work" from your blog, although it does happen. For example, Colleen was approached by a prospect who initially read her writing on www.marketingmixblog.com, where Colleen posts regularly, then followed a link to the site where she promotes her design services. The prospect very quickly hired Colleen to design a logo and web site for his new business.

Tina says her blog is her best self-promotional tool, though that was not her intention when she started it. Thanks to her blog, she has received requests for proposal from prospects and has been interviewed by magazines and other blog writers. "A blog is an amazing way to start a professional relationship," Tina says. "From there, they look up my graphic design portfolio and see the opportunity to collaborate. I've even had a few situations where I meet someone, hand them my card and they look at me in disbelief and say, 'You are Swiss Miss?'"

More than a traditional web site, a blog has the potential to convey your design sensibility and who you are as a person. Tina's advice is this: "Keep it real. Don't blog just simply to promote your services, or even worse, to cash in on advertising money. Readers will sense it right away if you sell out. Be passionate about your blog. Be consistent. Kept it fresh."

Driving Traffic to Your Site via Paid Search

You know those little text ads or sponsored links that appear on the right side of the screen when you do a search on a search engine? That's pay-per-click (PPC), sometimes known as "paid search." Those ads are different every time someone searches. In fact, the specific ads are chosen (or "served") based on their connection to the search terms used.

So what if, when someone is looking for a designer and types "designer" into the search field, your ad and a link to your web site comes up? Sounds great, right?

Here's the general idea of how paid search works: You first determine a specific amount of money that you're willing to pay each time a person clicks on your link for a specific keyword. For example, you may bid twenty-five cents on the term "graphic design." Every time a user enters that keyword phrase during a search, your site may come up in the results, and if the user clicks on the link, you're charged twenty-five cents. If another company bidding on the same term is willing to spend more per click, their site shows up higher on the page of search results than your site does. You can adjust your bid on that term to come up higher, and then they may do the same and so on. That's one downside to pay-per-click: It takes time and lots of attention.

Dozens of services offer a paid search model, but it's best to start with one of the big guys, such as Google AdWords, the easiest, quickest and most user-friendly service. They'll walk you through the process of setting up your first campaign and choosing your keywords. They even have people you can speak to live if you need help on your first campaign.

However, the only way paid search works is when the keywords or keyword phrases are very specific instead of general. So if you choose a general term like "graphic design," you'll pay a lot for clicks that don't ever convert into actual prospects, much less paying clients. Whereas, if you use keyword phrases such as "annual report design, Monmouth NJ," you'll get fewer but higher quality clicks and it will cost you a lot less.

COLD CALLING

You hate cold calling, we know. That's fine. But it's still one of the most effective marketing tools for getting exactly the kind of work and the caliber of clients you want—rather than being forced to take whatever comes along. That's why the most successful design firms bite the bullet and do it. And that's why you should, too.

One of the reasons you may hate it is because you have unrealistic expectations when you're reaching out to new prospects. You may wish people would say, "I'm so glad you called. I have a very creative project with a generous budget that would be perfect for you." That rarely happens, so if that's what you're looking for, you're likely to get discouraged.

What can (and does) happen, if you've targeted your market correctly, is the people you call will be mildly interested in what you have to offer. That's a good thing. That's what you want.

Here's what could happen if you do make these calls: You could reach prospects, and they could express interest. Then you could send them something and follow up a week later. They could put you off, but, undeterred, you could follow up again. And they might eventually respond because they are, in fact, interested, it's just that their plate is full. From there, you could schedule an appointment, on the phone or in person, to discuss a project, submit a proposal and maybe even get the job.

And if you stay in touch throughout this process, not dropping the ball anywhere along the way, this could turn into something good for everyone. But it all starts with a phone call. So here are some dos and don'ts of cold calling:

- Do use a list with contact names. A list of companies without names will require more work to locate the right person, so spend your time researching and compiling a list of the actual contacts at the companies you seek to work with. This will shave a lot of time off the process.

- Do leave a voice mail message so they can be familiar with you for the next time you call. Don't leave too many messages. Two or three over the course of a month isn't excessive.

- Do give your phone number at the beginning and the end of your message. That way, if they want to write it down, they don't have to listen all the way through in order to get it.

- Don't leave a long message. Respect their time, say what you need to say and then hang up.

- Do leave your web site address in case they want to check you out before they call you back or before you call again.

- Do approach your initial calls from a research perspective. You don't have to speak to the actual person on the first call. In fact, it helps to make contact with the screener—receptionist, secretary or assistant—because he or she is the one who is likely to determine your fate. Don't try to bypass or deceive the screeners; instead, get them on your side. They can be your advocate, your connection. Give them power by asking for their help.

Here's what you want to find out:

- if they have a need for your services
- with whom you should speak (who makes the decisions)
- if they're happy with the company they're currently working with
- if they're not happy, why not

Start the conversation by saying, "I'm looking for some information. Perhaps you can help me." Wait for them to agree before you continue. "I'm wondering if you use outside design services and, if so, I'd like to send you samples of work we've done for companies like yours. Who would be the appropriate person to speak to about this?" People are often willing to help you if they can and, if the timing is right, this research call can turn naturally into a "sales call."

Here are some common reasons why you may not want to make cold calls:

- You don't like rejection.
- You don't want to sound like a telemarketer.
- You don't like calling strangers.
- You don't think they'll take your call.
- You don't think it's worth your time.
- You don't have time to wait for these relationships to evolve.
- You don't think it will be successful.

Notice one thing about this list of reasons: They're all pretty negative. And if you make cold calls, indeed if you conduct any marketing effort, with the negative belief that it isn't going to work, well then, by gosh, it won't. Of that, you can be sure.

A Real-Life Success Story

"Hi, this is Merideth Harte from 3+Co. We are a boutique design studio in New York run by three sisters. We specialize in design and art direction for book and music packaging. I'm guessing that you are probably swamped with what you have going on at this particular moment, but I'm wondering if you might be looking at portfolios?"

That's the opening line Merideth Harte has used when she has made cold calls, which, at times, has been one of the main components of 3+Co.'s marketing machine.

But why would Merideth do something as distasteful as cold calling? "We were ready to expand our client base," she says. "We considered hiring a PR firm, but we know our business better than anyone, and we know who we want to work with."

The three sisters already had a strong client list in publishing and music packaging, so they made a list of fifty prospects that they felt confident they were a good fit for. Merideth did some simple online research to find out who the art directors were. Then, she picked up the phone.

"To get through it sometimes took lots of repeat calling, once or twice a week," Merideth says. "I didn't always leave a message. I didn't want it to seem like I was stalking them. I would just randomly throw a stone to see if I could hit them. When I reached someone, I'd explain who we are and what we do. More times than not, they were familiar with work we had done for other publishers and packagers, and I got good feedback."

In fact, what she got were actual projects for companies like Barnes & Noble, Random House and Universal Music Group.

Here's how Merideth says she did it: "I'd take time every day and set the goal of making contact with three or four people. I'd keep a list of each prospect, where I was with each one, who was responsive, etc. A few weren't interested because they don't farm out work or already work with another design company. Sometimes they said, 'Call me in six months.' But often, our timing was perfect; I'd reach someone who said, 'I really need someone now. Come right in,' or 'Where have you been and why don't I already know you?'"

"As soon as we got one positive response, it started to snowball," Merideth says. "You really can get what you wish for. You make a good connection with one client, and that leads to other jobs."

So what's the trick to making the cold calling work? According to Merideth, "Once you get the initial interest from someone, you think, 'Hey, it's not so bad. I can do this.' It's a matter of bolstering your confidence and not being overwhelmed."

Timing is everything when it comes to marketing. The more often your marketing machine gets the word out there, the higher your chances of being in the right place at the right time.

When you are introducing yourself to a new market, it helps to try out your approach on five to ten "practice prospects."

These are companies in the industry you're targeting with the same general needs as your top prospects, but you are less interested in them. They may not be as big, as well-connected, as promising for future business, as glamorous, as challenging, as lucrative, as intimidating or as desirable.

Whatever the reason, experimenting on practice prospects lowers your stress so you can perfect your pitch. With your practice prospects, you can work out the kinks in your script and figure out exactly what to say, which of their needs to emphasize and which of your services or products to highlight. You also can practice being more assertive and asking for the business. Without the stress, you will market yourself with more grace and less panic. You may even enjoy it. And who knows, your practice prospects may even sign on with you.

PROMOTIONAL MATERIALS

Even if you've got a beautiful web site out there in cyberspace, you still need tangible material that you can send to prospects so that it lands with a thud on their desks. This is much more effective than sending a link or even an attachment via e-mail (unless they specifically ask for that) because e-mail is ephemeral and your message could easily get buried at the bottom of the inbox.

If you can send actual samples of work you've done for other clients, that is ideal. But you may have only a few samples and none to spare if you're not thinking about your marketing as you negotiate your contracts.

Dani Nordin, who runs a design firm in Boston called the zen kitchen, usually negotiates for an additional twenty-five samples of every print project she designs for clients. By the time she runs out, the project has outlived its useful life. Says Dani, "Now that I'm starting to go after larger clients, though, I'm going to start sending actual physical samples. It really sends the message a lot better."

Show Instead of Tell

As a designer, you might not be able to offer a tangible sample of your work, but you might be able to use your site as an opportunity to show prospective clients what you can do by using some be-fore-and-after samples (with your previous clients' permission, of course). Or you can offer a critique of their existing materials and a few recommendations of what you would do if you were to improve on them.

The point is, you're always going to have a better connection when you get your prospects engaged in the process. And what better way to engage people than to give them a feel for how you could improve their businesses?

The best way to show clients what you can do and how you do it is by:

1. showcasing a portfolio with past clients' work
2. listing out client testimonials with client names, company names and dates intact
3. doing some case studies on a web site or blog and having links to download the case studies as PDFs

CALL FIRST OR SEND FIRST?

Should you call your prospects before sending them something, or send them something and then call? A debate rages on this question and there's no right answer. However, if you don't have the name of the person who buys creative services, always make a research call first to get that information. You'll never be able to follow up on a letter sent via snail mail to a title, such as "Corporate Marketing Director."

If you do have a contact name but no connection to the person, then also call first to make sure that person is a qualified prospect for your services. If they're not and you send them an expensive package (or even a simple letter), you've wasted much more time than you would have spent making the initial research call.

The only time to send something first is when you have the name of someone you are sure buys design services *and* you have a marketing piece that will really stand out from the clutter.

Erin L. Ferree, of elf design in northern California, sends out recipe cards with a cake recipe and the tagline "elf design makes marketing a piece of cake."

"While it doesn't always land new jobs," says Erin, "it gets people interested in my method of keeping in touch. I'm always top of mind when a project does come up. And people actually ask when my next mailing is coming out!"

Now that you have five strong marketing tools to work with, how will you use them to actually reach out and make contact? And will you let the common dilemma of not knowing what to say get in your way of reaching out?

One of the biggest obstacles to marketing is not time or money; it's not knowing what to say. But you can't come this far and then let that question prevent you from making contact with your prospects, whether you're making a cold call, following up with someone you met at a networking event or calling a referral from your best client. In this chapter, you'll learn all about what to say to prospects and clients in all sorts of marketing situations: in person, on the phone and online.

IN PERSON

Here's the thing about networking: It's nothing more than talking to people. But, for some reason, many people have trouble doing that. Whether it's not knowing what to say or imagining that someone else doesn't want to talk to you, something seems to get in the way of simple communication between two people.

It doesn't have to be that way. There are strategies you can use and preparation you can do to get ready for these conversations.

Reaching Out at a Networking Event

First of all, arrive early. If you wait until most of the attendees are already there, it will seem like everyone is already engaged in conversation (which isn't usually the case—it just may look that way), and it won't be as easy to find your way in. By arriving early, you can greet others as they arrive and engage them in conversation before they find someone else to talk to.

When you arrive at an event, what do you do first? Sign in, pay your money, get your nametag, right? It's not too early to start marketing yourself. Instead of trying to get away with as little interaction as possible, start connecting right away with whoever is there. So if you're signing in, that means introducing yourself to the person behind that little table and letting her know this is your first event.

This connection is a good idea because she is likely to be very involved in the group and can introduce you to people. She might hand you off to someone who will make you feel at home. After all, she wants you to have a good experience and come back to another meeting. Also, if your first interaction is a positive one, it will relieve your anxiety considerably so the next one will be that much easier. It could very well be smooth sailing from that moment on, all because of that first interaction you initiated.

Your nametag

If you have registered in advance (and if the group is organized), they will have a nametag ready for you. The size of the type may be really small or it may only have your name and nothing else, which isn't very useful from a marketing point of view, but you don't have much control over what's on it.

If you write your own nametag, focus on doing the following:

- Make sure your name is legible and written with a thick marker, if possible, so it's visible from afar and others don't need to squint or lean in close to read it.

- In bold, easy-to-read letters, include your name, your professional designation and your firm name.

- Put your web address on your nametag. It will be a conversation starter and will plant a little seed, encouraging those you meet to visit your web site.

As for where on your body to put your nametag, there's no "right" place. Some people say put it on the right because people read from left to right. Others argue for placing it on the left so that, if you're shaking hands with your right, they'll have a clear line of sight to your nametag. Just make sure it's visible; that's most important.

Where to sit

Despite the fact that the purpose of a networking event is to meet other people, many people just sit and wait for the networking to happen to them, rather than being proactive and initiating conversations. If this is your tendency, realize it early and do something different.

You may notice people scattered around the room, one lone person in each row of chairs or at each table. Instead of doing the same, choose one person, approach him and say, "Do you mind if I join you?" Then introduce yourself and you'll be off into conversation land. (And if not, read on for what to say.)

If the event is a presentation where you may have a chance to ask questions, sit near the front. That way, the presenter is more likely to call on you, and you may even have a chance to tell the group who you are and what you do.

It sometimes helps to attend an event with a friend or colleague—but once you've got your nametags on, go your separate ways. It's too easy to clump together, which discourages others from approaching you. Many opportunities to make new contacts are lost because people sit with their cohorts or with the same "safe" buddies every time. Make it a habit to sit with people you don't know. If one of your important clients or contacts is at the meeting, sit with him or her, but make sure you are seated at a table with strangers as well.

If you do bring a friend, split up to meet people and then introduce those people to each other. Or stay together and approach loners in the room and say, "Have you met [friend's name]? She has this great company." It is easier to brag about your friend as a way to introduce her. Being introduced by someone else makes conversation easier. Be sure to give quality introductions to your colleagues. Practice the introductions in advance.

Once you've started attending a particular meeting regularly and you feel comfortable, take a more active role as one of the hosts—formal or informal. All you have to do is stand near the door so you can greet people and introduce yourself as they walk in, making them feel comfortable and welcome. Or if you're at a table with others, become a "table moderator" and suggest that everyone introduce themselves and exchange business cards.

Who to talk to

Be random about where you sit or whom you approach. Do you have the bad habit of imagining you can tell, simply by a person's outfit or facial expression, whether they need design services? Of course, you know that you can't tell much about a person's needs by their wardrobe, so this strategy is a particularly ineffective one. So don't judge. Just sit next to someone randomly and see what happens.

Look for wallflowers. Instead of trying to break into conversations that are already in progress, find someone who is sitting or standing by himself and simply introduce yourself. Do it even if he looks like he doesn't want to be approached. The outward standoffishness may merely be a cover for discomfort (as yours may be).

Ask for introductions. If you see someone you'd like to meet, don't stand there wishing they would magically know that and come up to you. Ask someone (such as one of the group's staff members or the director of the group) to introduce you. Don't hesitate to do the same if you notice, on the attendance list or in the display of waiting nametags, that someone you'd like to meet is scheduled to attend.

HOW TO JOIN AN ONGOING CONVERSATION

Sometimes it may seem as though everyone is already in a conversation and no one is available to talk to you. What do you do?

Join in. Whether people are standing around chatting or sitting around a table, you can join in. While this may not be appropriate in other environments, in a networking environment, it is expected. Here's how to join a conversation:

Look for a physical opening. If there is a chair available, sit down, smile and listen to the person who is speaking. Generally, people will acknowledge your presence without interrupting the speaker. You should be unobtrusive yet present, so that when there is a conversational opening, you can introduce yourself and become part of the conversation. When there's a break in the conversation, say, "May I join you?" or "This looked like a lively conversation so I thought I'd join in."

What to say

This is one of the biggest obstacles for most people. You're fine once you're in a conversation; getting in is the challenge.

Some environments are easier than others. There will no doubt be events or parties where you just don't feel welcomed or in the mood to chat. Try to get over that by using your conversation skills and topics.

Use your blurbs (see chapter three) to exchange the basics, but don't focus on yourself. Instead, become interesting, which means become a good conversationalist. This includes listening well and bringing ideas, topics, questions, projects and your own challenges to discuss.

Interesting things are probably constantly happening to you. Do you take notice of them? You should, if your goal is to become a good conversationalist. All you have to do is take notice, remember the anecdote and then bring it up the next time you're in a networking situation.

Here are a few example topics to use as conversation starters:

- **Current events.** You may want to stay away from politics, but you can always talk about the latest scientific discovery, award recipients and sports tournaments. Movies are generally safe territory and quickly give you a good idea of what kind of person you're talking to.

- **Facts you've learned or books you've read.** Bring up a novel, biography or especially a business book that you've read, and share a bit of what you've learned.

- **Personal stuff.** If you have a new pet or are thinking of getting one, bring it up. If you're dealing with health issues and are looking for a particular resource, bring it up if you are comfortable doing so. If you were recently summoned to jury duty, bring it up.

- **When in doubt, talk about the food.** If there is a buffet, stand by it and make recommendations to anyone who approaches about what's good (or bad). But be sure to keep your hands free to shake hands and exchange business cards.

How to get out of a conversation

Some people have no trouble getting into conversations; it's getting out of them that presents the problem. So if you don't start conversations for fear of not being able to stop them, here are a few strategies to experiment with:

- **Get a refill.** If there's food or drink involved in the event, you can always say, "I think I need a refill." Or you can smile and say, "Excuse me. I need another one of those Swedish meatballs."

- **Involve another person.** Another escape is to introduce another person into the conversation. Then say, "Excuse me while I let you two get to know each other."

- **Stand up.** Sometimes you don't have to say anything. Just stand up! Your conversation partner is likely to take the nonverbal cue.

- **Hand them your card.** When you are ready to move on, hand the other person your business card, smile warmly and say, "I've enjoyed chatting with you. I'm going to mingle a bit. But let's stay in touch."

  - "I've really enjoyed meeting you, but since this is a networking event, I've set myself a goal to meet at least three people tonight. But let's stay in touch."

  - "I don't want to monopolize you. I'll let you talk to some other folks now. Let's stay in touch."

  - "I need to run, but let's exchange cards so we can keep in touch."

  - "Will you please excuse me? I see someone I need to chat with." Then leave quickly before they can tag along. This works well in a crowd (for obvious reasons).

- **Check on something.** Glance at your watch and say, "Excuse me, I need to make a quick phone call to check in with the [babysitter, boss, sick spouse … whatever is believable]."

Setting the Foundation for a Follow-Up

Have you ever met a bunch of people at an event, then arrived back at your office ready to do the follow-up and promptly begun staring into space, not knowing what to say?

Well, maybe it's because you didn't set the foundation for that follow-up while you were talking. One important tactic is to keep in mind, as you're talking, that you are looking for something to say in your follow-up. As soon as it hits you, make a note of it on the back of the person's card.

Here are a few ideas about how to make a connection with another person and simultaneously set the foundation for your follow-up:

- Don't talk about the weather, because beyond "It sure was cold yesterday," it is a very ineffective topic for follow-up.

- Find something in common. It can be personal or professional, but finding a topic of interest in common is a perfect way to reach out later (and more than once). When you come across something related to the topic, whether it's an idea or an event or an article or an opportunity, you can pass it along.

- Learn something new from one another. It may be uncomfortable, but strive to ask questions that lead in a direction you are unfamiliar with. For example, let's say you meet someone who mentions racing cars. Even if that's a topic you wouldn't normally be interested in, ask a few questions and learn a few things both about car racing and about the person. You can use that information later when you come across something related, and it will strengthen the initial connection. You can do this with any topic.

- Offer an idea, a contact or some other resource. As you're learning about this new person and his or her interests, search your mind for something or someone that would be a good connection. The follow-up is simply: "Here's the information I promised." This shows you're reliable, too.

- Find a project to collaborate on. This won't be possible with everyone, but if you are open to it, it may be possible with some people you meet. Listen for projects that might dovetail with something you've been thinking about. See if you can to take a few steps in that direction together.

Bring this list to your next event (business or personal), and see how much more productive your exchanges can be.

Staying Organized

One of the main reasons people fail to promote themselves properly is disorganization. Have you ever failed to follow up with an excellent prospect because you couldn't find his or her business card?

It's essential both to remember the conversation you've had with someone so you can follow up on it later, and to keep all the details (both physical and intangible) in order so you don't waste a lot of time searching. That's why it's essential to have a follow-up system in place that kicks in with the first moment of contact. Here are some ways to keep organized at a networking event:

- Wear a jacket with pockets. Keep your business cards and a pen in your left pocket and put any cards you get into your right pocket (or vice versa). That way, you won't be fumbling to find your cards or accidentally hand a new contact someone else's card.

- Try the top and bottom of the stack trick. Keep a stack of your cards in one pocket and as you collect them from new contacts, put those at the bottom of the stack. Just be sure you have enough of your own that you don't start giving away other people's business cards.

One-on-One Meetings

The ultimate goal of all the reaching out so far is to get "face time" with someone so you can learn more about his or her needs and show what you can do. Part of your follow-up to a networking event can be the request to meet for coffee or to show your portfolio.

The goal of these "getting to know each other" meetings is to find out as much as you can about the prospects, including their businesses, their needs and their history. It's a research experience, not a sales call. Keep in mind that some people will be open to this, and others won't have time to spend unless there's a potential project on the table. Don't take anything personally.

If they do have time for a networking meeting, go armed with questions. Do your research on the company. Google them and find out everything you can about their history. Read their web site as thoroughly as you can and refer to things you've read during the conversation. This shows you are serious and well-prepared, which are excellent qualities no matter what the situation.

Sometimes this meeting can take the form of a portfolio presentation, so always have your portfolio of samples handy and available, in case things start moving in that direction.

Be careful, though, because often the focus falls too much on the portfolio and past work, rather than on future and potential work. The portfolio in itself is not as important as how you present it. So here are some tips to make sure you get the most out of these one-on-one meetings:

- Don't hand the portfolio over to your prospects and watch silently as they flip the pages. Instead, sit next to them and talk them through each project, describing all you can about who the clients were, what their challenges were and how you helped them figure it all out.

- Don't recite your monologue about the work in your portfolio without letting the prospects get a word in edgewise. Instead, offer a bit of information and then pause to see if your prospects have a question or comment about it. Keep the conversation going this way as long as you can.

- Don't let your portfolio take center stage. Essentially, your portfolio is a prop, not the star of the show. Some prospects will want to spend time admiring your work; others won't even ask to see it, but instead will launch into a speech about what they need. You must be prepared for either situation and let the prospects determine the direction of the conversation.

- Don't go into a long dissertation about yourself and your work (when your company was founded, blah, blah, blah). Instead, give the basics (such as how long you've been in business, your main area of expertise and types of clients you work best with), and make it short and sweet.

An effective portfolio is a springboard, helping you make a smooth transition into a conversation with your prospect about what they need and what you can do for them. The best-case scenario is one in which your prospect sees something that gets the conversation going in the direction of an actual project, leaving your old work in the dust.

"YOU NEED SERIOUS HELP"

How do you approach clients you think need serious help and pitch your services without offending them?

First, you must find out what they think. Design in particular is very subjective. They may think what they've got is good enough and not that important. Or they may love what they have. Or they may know it's horrible but just haven't focused their attention on it and taken the time to find someone they trust to help. That may be you. They may be looking and waiting for you to call.

So before you give your opinion, find out where they stand, and base your response on that. Consider offering a critique of their existing materials or process, which you can then use as a more formal way of not only presenting your opinion, but also demonstrating the value of your expertise.

ON THE PHONE

Many people who have no trouble meeting new prospects in person seem to have an abject fear of calling them on the phone. Not being able to see the other person can be intimidating. If you can't see her face or her body language, how will you know what she's really thinking? (In reality, you can't know what she's thinking even if you can see her very clearly.)

Should I Use a Script?

Whether you're making warm or cold calls, it helps to start with a script as you prepare for the call. But a script is not helpful during the actual call for the simple reason that the other person doesn't have a copy of your script.

What works better is to have a list of talking points—the three to five things that you don't want to forget to ask or say. Then, during the call, just respond to what the other person says. If you get flustered, it doesn't matter. Just keep going. Use your talking points as a prompt, but don't get too attached to them.

You might also want to keep a "cheat sheet" of your best qualities and success stories by the phone, in case none come readily to mind.

And practice, practice, practice.

SIMPLE SCRIPT FOR AN INTRODUCTORY CALL

Hi, I'm Ilise Benun. You don't know me, but I see your name here in the directory of the New Jersey Business Marketing Association. I'm a member, too. Do you have a moment?

Wait for them to give you permission to continue or find out when it's best to call back.

I work with luxury travel companies on their trade show marketing. You may not be the right person to speak with, but I'm wondering if your company works with outside designers on that. (If not, who is?)

Wait for a response. If they seem at all positive or open, make your offer to send materials. If they say yes, get their address. Then, make one more offer:

One more thing: We publish a free monthly e-zine about trade show marketing. I'd be happy to add you to the list. The next one will go

out in a couple weeks. Would you like to receive that? If so, all I
need is your e-mail address.

If you don't get through, leave a voice mail message.

Hi, I'm Ilise Benun, and you don't know me, but I work with com-
panies like yours, such as [drop names] on trade show marketing
materials. I would like to send samples of work we've done for com-
panies like yours. If that sounds good to you, all you have to do is
call me back at [phone number]. Otherwise, I will try to reach you
again. You can also find us online at [spell out your web address].
And if you're not the right person to speak to about this, I'd appreci-
ate it if you would point me in the right direction.

NETWORKING ONLINE

More and more, business is moving online, and that includes networking. So in addition to knowing what to say in person, you need to figure out what to say online so that you're promoting yourself while also providing useful information to people who may one day become clients.

Social Networking Web Sites

You've probably heard of LinkedIn (www.linkedin.com), the online business community of millions of people. It's like MySpace for business. Maybe you've received invitations to "join" a colleague's network. Perhaps you've even joined—it's free. If so, you can take advantage of the system when you follow up with new people you meet.

LinkedIn is based on the idea that weak ties tend to be more important than strong ties. In his best-selling book *The Tipping Point*, Malcolm Gladwell quotes sociologist Mark Granovetter on the strength of weak ties: "Your friends, after all, occupy the same world that you do. They might work with you, or live near you, and go to the same churches, schools or parties. How much, then, would they know that you wouldn't know? Your acquaintances, on the other hand, by definition occupy a very different world than you. They are much more likely to know something that you don't."

You can use the LinkedIn network to make connections with people who know the people you know, who can then become prospects for you with potentially lucrative projects.

After a networking event, instead of using regular e-mail to reach out to the people with whom you've exchanged business cards, use the LinkedIn invitation feature to do double duty: Follow up and invite them into your network. If your new connection accepts your invitation, you both have a tangible reminder of your connection. Plus, you also have access to their network of contacts.

Here are a few other helpful networking sites:

- www.ryze.com—With a 500,000 members in 200 countries, this free networking site aims to keep people in touch worldwide. The "Entrepreneurs" network on this site has nearly 9,000 members.

- www.tribe.net—Much like Craigslist, this site is city-oriented. You can use it to network with people in your own community, or to reach members around the country.

- www.doostang.com—This free, invitation-only "career community" is a place where you can connect with others through your friends and colleagues.

Discussion Lists

If the ideal marketing moment is when your prospects are in their moment of need for your services, how do you find them at precisely that moment? One way is to go where people go when they're looking for help. One of those places is to the Internet, in particular, to e-mail discussion groups and online forums.

I'm not talking about chat rooms, where little of value is exchanged. Viable business forums and e-mail discussion lists, however, offer an environment where people who need help post questions, while others reply with ideas, resources and links to sites with more information.

Discussion list marketing is one of those great guerrilla marketing tactics because it's free and effective (especially in niche markets of almost any kind) when you do it right. Plus, it doesn't require much time—just consistency and generosity. Contributing regularly to these discussions can increase your odds of being in the right place at the right time with the right tidbit of information. The best discussions are very specific to a topic or industry.

These discussions take place in a couple of different formats. Some are web sites that you have to go to in order to participate in the discussion, many of which have an e-mail alert system that will let you know when someone has posted to the group or on a particular topic.

Others are listservs, which include e-mail messages that are delivered to a group with the postings from everyone and instructions on how to respond to the questions. These are the most convenient because they are delivered directly to your inbox, either one at a time or in digest format. That way, you don't have to remember to go to a web site.

Blogs are a recent addition to the online discussion world. In fact, writers often use blogs to gather material, so if you have contributed an idea or tip to someone else's blog, you may be asked for permission to be included in a book or e-book, which couldn't hurt your marketing efforts.

Once you've chosen one or two discussion lists, subscribe and then lurk long enough to see whether your prospects are in fact accessible through the group. If not, unsubscribe and find another. Don't waste your time on lists where people do nothing but argue and vent. Find a list where people are actually sharing useful information and join in the conversation.

If someone submits a post looking for design services, send a brief and polite note directly to him or her (not to the entire list) explaining how you could help and asking if he or she would like to see samples.

TIPS FOR MAKING A SPLASH ON DISCUSSION LISTS

- Don't promote yourself overtly. Most lists have strict rules about how and when members can promote themselves, so read the rules and follow them. The best way to sell yourself is to show what you know, share valuable information and answer people's questions.

- Use your e-mail signature for self-promotion. Include your tagline, refer to yourself as an "expert in X" and provide a link to your web site.

- Contribute in a positive way to the discussion. That means you should:
  - ask a question where the answer is likely to interest others or stimulate discussion
  - answer a question meaningfully

- introduce some new (preferably useful) piece of information, insight or opinion to an ongoing discussion
- identify a resource (e.g., article, book, web site, event) of interest to the list
- relate an interesting story, anecdote or opinion that stimulates a discussion thread

Where to find online discussions

Start with the trade publications read by your target market. Many of them offer an online forum or listserv as an added benefit for readers. For example, *Fast Company* magazine has a global readers' network on their site at www.fastcompany.com/cof/.

Check out the trade associations for your target market; they often have discussion forums on various topics pertinent to the members. For example, if your market is higher education and universities, go to the Council for Advancement and Support of Education (www.case.org) and look for their "communications" listserv in the resources section.

There are lots of forums for designers—including the HOW Magazine Forum (http://forum.howdesign.com) and About.com's forum for graphic design (http://graphicdesign.about.com/mpboards.htm). This is not necessarily where you'll meet your prospects, but you can engage in discussions with other designers, which can sometimes lead to work.

Now your marketing machine is ready, and you have all the scripts and talking points you need to go out there and start talking to people. Remember that the key is follow-up, which keeps the conversation going after you've made initial contact.

CHAPTER 6
HOW SHOULD I FOLLOW UP?

"Out of sight, out of mind" never happened as fast as it does these days.

That's exactly why it's important to be in your prospects' faces. If you are, they will be more likely to think of you and send a project your way. You can't expect that if they want you, they'll just call you, especially if they haven't heard from you in a while. That's why it's your responsibility to follow up and stay on their radar. The number one way you could get in your own way is by neglecting to follow up on the prospects that come your way.

FOLLOW UP WITH A PERSONAL MESSAGE

Because there's almost as much junk e-mail as junk snail mail, the same problem exists for both: How can you send messages that will actually rise above the clutter?

The same answer applies to both, also: Make it personal. When corresponding with a prospect, you may think you should be formal, perhaps to show professionalism. But in an e-mail, formal language often comes across as dry, or even hostile. Your e-mail messages should be respectful, but they should have a personal and personable tone of voice. For example, "thanks so much" instead of "thank you very much" can create a more relaxed relationship. The differences are small and subtle, but significant.

Here are some examples:

1. Follow-up to a cold or warm call

- **Formal:** Don, I am following up on the materials we forwarded to your attention. Did you receive them? Do you have any questions?

- **Informal:** Hi, Don. Just making sure you got the samples we sent. Maybe it's still in a pile of mail? And I'm wondering whether you have questions about the work or any projects coming up that we can quote on. Let me know.

2. Follow-up to a meeting at a networking event

- **Formal:** Cindy, when we met last week at the Townville Chamber Business Card Exchange, you expressed interest in my design services, so I wonder if you'd like to receive our promotional package.

- **Informal:** Great to meet you last week at the Chamber event, Cindy. Since you showed interest in what we do, may I send you some samples of our work? If so, just hit reply with your address and we'll send them along.

3. Follow-up and touching base with new work

- **Formal:** Here's a link to a web site where you will find some new work we recently completed.

- **Informal:** Cindy, just wanted to point you to some new work we recently completed.

Another way to make your e-mail messages more personal is to refer to something that you discussed with this person or to something you know they would recognize. Ask about their kids, vacation, holidays. Find out what's important to them as a person, and use that information to build your relationship with them via e-mail.

Ask a Question in Your E-Mail Follow-Up

Statistics vary on how many marketing efforts—or "touches"—it takes to turn a new prospect into a client, but the average is more than five, sometimes as many as nine. That's right, nine times that you need to reach out, one way or another, educating your market about how you can help them, reminding them that you exist, helping them get to know you and building trust before they sign on the dotted line. That's why following up must be the engine of your marketing machine.

Here is an example of a follow-up message sent by cartoonist Lloyd Dangle, creator of *Troubletown*, after he met a prospect at the Licensing Show in New York City:

Subject line: CORPORATE SLIME = CANDY?

Dear Steven,

No, I'm NOT calling YOU corporate slime! I'm writing to remind you of the design of a greedy, power-mad suit that you saw—and expressed interest in—at the Licensing Show.

My notes say that your reaction was, "YOWEEEE! I could make candy out of that." (I added the YOWEEEE myself; you didn't actually say that.)

I'm reaching out to you to see if we might make this or another project happen this year. I want to pitch you ideas, but only in a productive way that suits you. Please let me know which you prefer:

- *E-mail me samples*
- *Mail me samples*
- *Call me at around_____am/pm*
- *The time of year we look at designs is: a) anytime, b)_____*
- *Other:_____*
- *No thanks, you're not the kind of SLIME we work with here.*

Thank you for your time, and keep an eye on your snail mail for something from me soon.

Sincerely,
Lloyd Dangle

Notice how, in this follow-up e-mail message, Lloyd reminds his prospect of his interest, expresses his eagerness to work together and then asks how he should stay in touch.

Asking a question is a good strategy because it gives your prospect something specific to respond to.

How to Use Voice Mail as a Follow-Up Weapon

When calling your prospects, you're going to get voice mail—accept that as a fact. These days, people screen their calls or simply don't answer. If you reach secretaries or receptionists and they offer you a choice between leaving a message with them and leaving a voice mail message, take the voice mail. You have much more control over what message gets through if you convey it yourself.

Give your prospect or contact as much information as possible about who you are and what it's like to work with you. Your voice can play a part in that. The sound of your voice, your tone and your cadence are all factors in creating rapport. Your prospect will hear not only your voice and your words, but also your inflection. The sound of your voice can strengthen connections with people who receive only e-mail from you, helping them better understand who and how you are—ideally, relaxed and friendly rather than anxious and abrupt.

WHAT TO SAY ON YOUR VOICE MAIL MESSAGE

Here are a few guidelines to follow when leaving a voice mail message:

- Be brief. Don't ramble on. Use a script, but practice enough so it doesn't sound like you're reading.

- Be conversational, and use inflection in your voice.

- Start with your "headline"—the core idea, your question, the goal of your message —and then continue with details, in case they don't listen all the way through.

- Give your phone number at the beginning and at the end of your message.

- Tell them what you'll do next (and be sure to do it).

THE FOLLOW-UP PROCESS, STEP BY STEP

Step 1: Send an e-mail message right away.

Scenario 1: You meet someone at an event, make a good connection, find out a little about her business and promise to send a link related to what you were discussing with her. She expresses interest in your services, but it's not clear whether she's an actual prospect.

As soon as you get back to your office, follow up your initial conversation with an e-mail message. This will build on the momentum of the conversation, while the conversation is still fresh in your mind and you are still fresh in her mind. If too much time passes before you follow up, the conversation may blur with another one she had around the same time or at the same event.

In your e-mail message, do the following:

- Thank her for her interest, for taking the time to speak with you and for anything else she went out of her way to do.

- Express what you understand to be the challenge she faces. Use her language as much as possible. For example, if she said she needs help to "grow her business," use that phrase in your comments to her, instead of any other words you might use to express the same thing.

- Refer to an experience or project in your background that supports your claim that you are the right person to help. (You can do this even if she isn't a prospect for your business.)

- Offer the information or link you mentioned in the conversation. Also include a link to your web site and, if at all possible, to a relevant case study or article, based on what you know so far about her challenge. This shows that you were listening.

- Get her into your loop. Ask if she'd like to receive your e-mail newsletter or tips or postcards or whatever your system is for keeping in touch with your network. And even if that system isn't entirely in place, you can still sign people up and get their permission to stay in touch. In fact, when enough people say yes, that will help motivate you to do it even more.

Scenario 2: You meet someone who is clearly a prospect for your services. He gives you his card and says, "I'd like to talk to you further." How is your follow-up message different than the follow-up for scenario 1?

It's even more important in this type of follow-up to use persuasive copy that focuses on the benefits of working with you.

Follow this simple three-step formula: (1) State with confidence what you can do, (2) list three or more things (and the benefits of each) he'll get by working with you, and (3) close with a testimonial and a way to keep in touch.

Here's an example:

Hi, Tom.

It was great to meet you at the HOW Design Conference.

I am confident I can help you create a plan to get your new business off the ground. The Marketing Mentor program would be an effective way to do that because it provides the three things you need most at this point in your business:

- *A plan. Together, we will create a marketing plan that is tailored to your needs and your most lucrative target market.*

- *Accountability. I will keep you on track with our weekly phone calls so your marketing doesn't get put on the back burner, eliminating the feast-or-famine syndrome forever.*

- *Objective feedback. My twenty years of experience helping people just like you promote their services means you won't waste time and money making beginner's mistakes.*

I'll call you next week to continue the conversation, but in the meantime, you'll receive my free e-mail newsletter, Quick Tips from Marketing Mentor. *Here's what another writer said about the tips: "Your online newsletter is absolutely terrific. You combine extremely valuable content with style and personality. Fabulous job!"*

Step 2: Send materials in the mail.

As soon as you send the e-mail message, put together a package of materials to send in the mail. At this trust-building stage of the process, your objective is to create the strongest impression possible to show prospects you are serious, professional and qualified.

Expand the text of your e-mail message into a short letter that builds on and reiterates your ideas. Don't worry about repeating yourself. Repetition ensures that they get the message.

Enclose a brochure, samples or anything else that will help support your position that you are credible and qualified. Put together the most professional package you can, with some of the elements on the following page. (Don't include them all; you don't want to overwhelm your prospects at this point. Just give them a little bit more to chew on.)

- a one-sheet or list of your services
- a biography or other background piece about you
- a case study of a project you've worked on
- article clips about you or written by you (if possible)

For contacts who aren't necessarily prospects or who aren't ready to receive (or need) your information packet, brochure or other detailed materials, send a simple, handwritten note on your letterhead or a note card. Enclose your business card, even if you have already given it to them.

A personal note really shows you took extra time to get in touch. People notice, and it can really set you apart. Plus, people just love getting mail that isn't junk!

To top it off, use an unusual stamp to make your mail stand out from the pile. It is another subtle way to show style and personality.

Step 3: Call to make sure they received the materials.

Don't ever assume anything: that they received your materials, that they took the time to look at what you sent, and especially that if they are interested, they'll pick up the phone to call you for the next step.

They may, but don't assume they will. It is your responsibility to follow up.

One week after you send your materials, call to confirm they received what you sent. Ask if they've had a chance to look through it yet. (If you don't reach them, leave this message via voice mail and also e-mail.) If they have looked at it, their need for your help may be urgent and the process may go quickly. If they haven't, don't take it personally. Just know that they're probably in information-gathering mode and will need to get beyond that before they're ready to talk further or meet. Adjust your follow-up schedule accordingly. But stay in close touch through this part of the process because if you drop the ball, you may miss the window of opportunity.

Also, ask how they prefer to be contacted for follow-up. With this simple question, you can find out a lot of important information, such as their preferences or phobias for the phone, e-mail or snail mail. You might hear "Oh, I never read e-mail" or "I always let voice mail screen my calls." Keep track of these preferences for each prospect, client and contact, and reach out accordingly.

Don't end the conversation until you find out when you should reach out again—then be sure to do so.

THE PERFECT TIME TO FOLLOW UP

You want your name to be fresh in your prospects' minds when you call them. If you call too soon, they may not have received your package yet—too late, and they may have forgotten about it. One week after sending your materials is a good time to follow up. If the information is sitting on their desks in a pile of unopened mail, your call will motivate them to look at it. You can even say, "I'll bet it's in a pile on your desk." Or even better, "I'll bet it's in that pile on the left." You'll probably get a chuckle and can move on from there.

Step 4: Follow up the meeting.

After a meeting, whether on the phone or in person, you'll have a much better idea of how close prospects are to engaging your services. Base your follow-up strategy on that information. If the challenge they're facing is a priority, they'll ask you for a proposal.

If they're not quite ready to commit to you, find out:

- what their decision-making process is
- what else they need from you
- when they'll be making a decision
- what you should do next

Then do what they say. Call when they tell you to call. That may be obvious, but people often forget or lose track of when they're supposed to call next. This is another reason to use a system to keep track of these important details. Plus, if you're marketing yourself properly, this prospect isn't the only one in your pipeline. Keeping track of the time frames for several prospects simultaneously requires discipline, organization and reliable tools.

As time goes by, you may have to remind these prospects of their interests and of the solutions you bring to their problem. Don't get discouraged if this drags on. It's easy to let the ball drop here, and most people will. Summon as much self-discipline as you need to stay focused on your goal and your commitment to the process.

Keeping in touch isn't all that hard, especially if you have a system or a "loop" in place. Here are a few ways to stay in touch:

- Call to check in on the status of the prospects' needs or projects.
- Send e-mail messages with links to relevant information or upcoming events of interest.
- Send updates about projects you're working on that may relate to theirs.
- Send relevant articles (ideally written by you, but not necessarily).

- Forward an idea or a resource you hear about at a conference or meeting that relates to their projects.

This strategy applies also when you have initiated contact with prospects who have a need but aren't "in pain" about it, and it's a matter of time before they will address the issue. This could take weeks or months (or more), but just keep in touch no matter what, to show them you're thinking of them and their problems.

NEW CONTACT FORM

Use the following list to gather information on and keep track of each new contact you meet.

Name:

Company:

Address:

Phone (office, cell, fax):

E-mail address:

Web address:

Where you met:

| What they do: |
| Their market: |
| Their current challenge: |
| Ideas you have for helping resolve it: |
| Resources you can offer: |
| Follow-up preferences: |

Dates for steps in the process:

    Step 1—E-mail follow-up:

    Step 2—Send materials:

    Step 3—Phone follow-up:

    Step 4—What's next:

If proposal is to be submitted:

    Date submitted:

Date they will make a decision:
Their decision-making process:
What else they need from you:
Next step:

YOU CAN'T FOLLOW UP WITHOUT A SYSTEM

We all have the best intentions when it comes to following up. But good intentions aren't usually enough. What you need is a system to keep track of what you did when, what they said when and any other important information you might need later.

If you don't have a system, each time you want to follow up with someone, you have to stop and think about what to say and what to send. Anything you have to think about is going to be put off until you have time to think, which doesn't come around too often in our fast-paced, multitasking world.

Your system doesn't have to be fancy or even high-tech. A simple tickler file will do—on paper or electronic—as long as it reminds you what to do when. Or you could just use a calendar on which you mark each call or schedule each marketing effort.

And there are lots of free, web-based tools available online, such as Highrise, a contact management system created by 37 Signals. (Find it at www.highrisehq.com.)

Once you've got your system in place, you'll have to get in the habit of using it. Integrating a new process into your routine will take some time, but it's the only way to get it into your day-to-day life.

Set aside time every week to do your follow-up, whether it's making calls, sending e-mail messages or forwarding an interesting article to everyone on your list. Do this to keep in touch with the prospects that you are nudging along the path toward working with you.

How Often to Follow Up

Alas, there are no rules to follow because each prospect is different. Your prospects will gladly tell you the best way to keep in touch—if you ask. To be on the safe side, make contact monthly or every other month, depending on how close they are to being ready.

How to Determine Which Are Your Best Leads

All prospects are not equal, and it's essential to know which are your best leads so that, when your business starts to take off, you know your priorities and don't drop the ball on the most promising future prospects. That, after all, is how the feast-or-famine syndrome starts.

The first thing to do is determine your prospect's rating. Here's one way to think about it:

C = prospects with a casual interest
B = prospects with a qualified need and a possible project

A   = qualified prospects with an actual project

A+ = prospects who have given you a verbal commitment but haven't yet signed on

Once you know where all your prospects stand on this scale, you can then determine the best way to contact each (and the proper frequency for each prospect). A creative professional typically pursues a "C" opportunity three or four times in the course of one month. However, you may try contacting a "B" opportunity a few more times (and for a bit longer), and an "A" opportunity even more persistently and for a longer period of time.

Be sensitive to each situation, and temper your persistence with your gut feeling. If the prospect in question travels a lot, or is an extremely busy executive, it's unlikely she will drop what she's doing when you call, but she still may want you to stay in touch.

Don't Stop Following Up

Turning prospects into clients is, quite simply, the natural result of a good, persistent follow-up. Although some business owners consider a prospect dead if no projects result after a year of follow-up, the really ambitious ones won't stop until they either get the job or find out there's no longer any job to get.

Some projects or prospects take years to come through and your "job" during that time is to keep nudging them along and check in consistently to see whether the problem persists and the prospect is still planning to get it solved. It's not unusual to have prospects who, for a year or two, don't have the budget to work with you.

There may also be prospects who are happy with the resource they're using but will eventually want to change. This is very common, for example, with design firms who do annual reports. Many corporations sign a three-year contract with a design firm for their annual reports. When that period ends, even when the relationship is a good one, they will move on to another design firm.

One design firm that specializes in annual reports has been pursuing several prospects for years. They see the process as planting seeds, and they have even gone so far as to suggest submitting a proposal when the prospect didn't ask for it and wasn't yet ready to change. They do this when it's a client they feel they could do a good job for and want an opportunity to show what they could do, how they would approach it and how much it would cost. Doing this proposal requires a lot of time and effort on their part, a risk certainly, but it also takes a lot of the guesswork out of the process for the prospect who, until then, hadn't seen anything more than past work.

When Is It Time to Back Off (But Not Give Up)?

There does come a point, however, when it's obvious that staying in touch every month is overkill. That's when it's time to stop the personal outreach and get them on auto-drip.

Ideally, your prospects will tell you that the project is on hold or has been taken off the table. However, they may not. It's best to find out what happened so you aren't hanging on indefinitely. If you can't reach your prospects, try to reach a colleague who can tell you the status of the project.

In any case, this is when your objective shifts from attempting to solicit a response to keeping your visibility high. The tenor of your messages should shift, too. Don't be so focused on getting them to respond; instead, stay upbeat, report good news and keep your name alive. What you want them to do is register your message.

Transfer these prospects to the semiannual category—you reach out personally twice a year. Announce finished projects or new clients garnered, let them know of upcoming press coverage you got that they may see (or better yet, let them know to watch their mailbox for a copy of it that you'll send along soon), or simply wish them a happy new year and reinforce your desire to work with them in the coming year.

In addition to the personal messages (and it's essential that these are truly personal rather than a mass e-mail message), make sure that they are on your list to receive your newsletter, postcard or some other regular contact from you.

When Is It Too Late to Follow Up?

The simple answer is: Never.

Following up is the key to growing your business. When and how you do it is up to you, but you can always do it. Saying it's too late to follow up is a cop out. There's no statute of limitations on follow-up. It's better to do it sooner rather than later, but it's never too late (unless your prospect is no longer alive, but even then, the project may still be alive).

The amount of time that has passed will determine what you say and how you say it. For example, if you met someone last month at a luncheon and haven't followed up yet, there's no need to feel bad or to apologize. Simply say, "I can't believe it's already been a month since we met. I'm finally catching up on my follow-ups and wanted to be sure and let you know how much I enjoyed our conversation."

Even if you met someone last year, you can still follow up—it's just that you may need to remind them who you are. Say something like, "I just found your card buried under a stack of papers and I hope you remember me. We met at the NIRI Conference and I was wearing a bright orange scarf, and we talked about chocolate and the Scarsdale Diet."

This is where those notes on the back of the card, as well as the "wear something unusual" strategy, come in handy.

Don't apologize. Unless you promised to get back to them with some information and didn't (in which case, it is appropriate to apologize), you really don't need to say you're sorry. After all, they haven't followed up with you, either.

And even if they have, we are so barraged with messages that people are much more forgiving if one slips through the cracks. Your job in reaching out is to fill in those cracks.

The Line Between Pestiness and Persistence

The main reason most people fail in the follow-up arena is because they give up too soon—way too soon. You don't want to be perceived as a pest, so you stop reaching out. How hard should you push? How many times should you reach out? How often is too often to call or e-mail? Are three times enough? Six times too many?

Alas, there is no rule.

The line between persistence and pestiness is a thin one, and it's a moving target. In other words, it depends on the day, on the prospects, on their needs and many other things you won't even get wind of.

Each of your prospects can tell you their preference, and often they will. If they say they're not ready, ask when and how they'd like you to follow up. You can even ask if they think it's worth your time to do so. Most often they will tell you the truth—but only if you ask.

ONGOING FOLLOW-UP

The only way to stay in touch with everyone in your network is with a regular marketing vehicle—something you do like clockwork, monthly or at least quarterly, and for which you don't have to reinvent the wheel every time.

An e-mail marketing campaign (see Chapter Four) is ideal here. It allows you to showcase your work, share your knowledge and build credibility, while also spreading the word about your services and distinguishing you from other designers. E-mail marketing also drives traffic to your web site in a much more reliable and controllable way than search engines do. And best of all, e-mail serves as a prompt for your recipients. When they get a message from you, it encourages them to respond. And all they have to do is click "reply."

G. Scott Souchock, principal of Seattle-based G.Scott!Design, does environmental graphic design for educational institutions. His e-mail newsletter, *Wayfinding 101*, offers "pithy, practical, informative, and often fun tips, stories, case studies, and examples about wayfinding, signage, and the world of environmental graphic design."

His list started small—just his clients and a few prospects—but has been growing steadily since he started his e-mail newsletter. He is always in list-building mode, asking people if they'd like to receive *Wayfinding 101* and remembering to include a link to a sample in the signature file in his regular e-mail correspondence.

Besides e-mail, there are other tools you can use to stay in touch regularly, such as a printed newsletter, a postcard series or a monthly calendar. But whatever tool you choose, make sure you use it consistently so everyone in your network can relax in the knowledge that you'll stay in touch with them.

If you do all of the marketing efforts recommended here, your marketing machine will be in full gear within six months, and soon you'll have people reaching out to you saying, "I've been getting your materials for a while now, and I'd like to talk about a project we have in mind."

That's when you have to start thinking about how to price your work.

PART TWO

PRICING

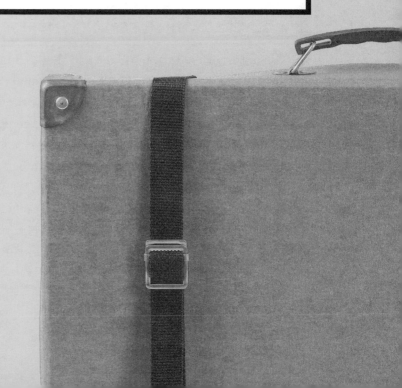

CHAPTER 7
HOW DO I MANAGE MY MONEY?

As in the marketing of your business, there are two aspects to the "pricing" side: how you deal with your own issues about money, and how you interact with your clients. Until your own issues—such as payment terms and policies—are resolved, you can't effectively begin to think about how those issues affect your clients. So, first about you.

HOW DO I DEAL WITH MY PERSONAL MONEY?

Are you detail-oriented about lines and shapes, but fuzzy when it comes to money? Do you balance your personal checkbook, or do you just write checks and pray your balance stays above zero? Do you know how much revenue you need to generate in order to pay your bills every month, or do you just cross your fingers and hope enough money comes in? Are the numbers clear in your head, or is it all a blur?

For many creative types, money is an obstacle to doing business. "I'm bad with numbers," is a common refrain and, frankly, a common excuse used to neglect essential business tasks like billing. Believing you are "bad with numbers" is often the excuse for ignoring situations that can imperil a business.

If your personal finances are not in order, your business finances won't be, either. If you aren't aware of your regular expenses, you won't have a way to assess whether you can afford the next computer upgrade or the next employee hire, and you won't know when and where to trim when you need to. Even if you hire someone to manage the financial aspect of your business, which you may be in a position to do, it's important that you stay involved and aware of the big picture.

YOUR MONEY MENTALITY

One fundamental aspect of the financial end of running a design business is the mental attitude you bring to the process.

Which of these statements is most familiar to you:

"I can't stand dealing with money."

    or

"This financial thing is a challenge, but I'm going to learn it and make it work for me."

How about these:

"I can't afford to spend money on marketing."

    or

"What do I need to do in order to afford the marketing I know I need to grow my business?"

It's up to you. You can choose between an open or closed mentality. Open is better and will facilitate the growth of your business. With this positive mental attitude as a foundation, you can begin planning your future.

YOU ARE IN THE DRIVER'S SEAT:
PLANNING AND MANAGING YOUR MONEY

Your business is there to feed you, and feed you well, if you want. But there is a lot you need to know about your business in order to get the financials right. That's what this chapter is all about.

Start by figuring out what you need financially. Then, go to your business and say, "Business, this is what I need." You must be willing to do the work required to have your business deliver this to you.

Robert Kiyosaki, best known as the author of *Rich Dad, Poor Dad*, says, "Failing to plan is planning to fail." When he talks about failing, he's not necessarily talking about going bankrupt. Another definition of failure is holding yourself back or staying static, and this is often the result of a lack of planning.

Planning involves knowing what systems and elements you need to have in place, such as:

- **The numbers.** From a financial standpoint, you must understand a few simple numbers—your basic overhead (what it costs to run your business, including your hourly rate), your profit (what you earn over and above your expenses) and your budgets (spending projections based on revenue projections)—before you can start pricing a project.

- **Bookkeeping, billing and collection.** It's essential to have a system in place so you can keep close track of where your time and money go. (There is software to do that; we recommend Function Fox.) Everything that comes in and goes out should be documented. You may need a bookkeeper to come in regularly to do bookkeeping or billing, or at least to oversee what you are doing and make sure you're doing it right.

- **Business policies, payment terms and conditions.** You are in the driver's seat here. Don't wait for your clients to tell you how to run your business. One of the benefits of being self-employed is that you get to determine how (and often how much) you want to be paid. You get to decide what to do when surprises occur, such as the cancellation of a job or twenty-five rounds of revisions. This must all be spelled out in advance and included in your contract.

- **The paperwork.** Memories are woefully inadequate, so don't even try to rely on yours when it comes to the agreements you make with your clients. Instead, set up a simple documentation system with templates for proposals, contracts, estimates, letters of agreement, schedules, timelines and change orders that your clients will sign off on. This sets a professional tone right from the beginning of any business relationship. If you fail to institute this process at the outset, it's much more challenging to put systems in place later on.

In order to set goals and determine a budget, you must work out not only what you need to earn, but also how that number translates into the number of clients you need, and how that translates into how much marketing you must do in order to achieve that.

In other words, how many proposals do you have to submit each month in order to make your numbers? How many calls (cold or warm) must you make to be asked for that number of proposals? How many prospects do you need in your pipeline in order to get that number of requests for proposals?

Without taking the time to work this out for yourself, it's unlikely you'll achieve your goals. Plus, without this information, you won't know when to step up your marketing, when to attend one more networking event, when to make a round of follow-up calls or when to send out an extra newsletter.

PELEG TOP'S PERSONAL MONEY MANAGEMENT SYSTEM

You can become an excellent money manager—it is a habit that can be learned. Here is a money management system that works for Peleg Top. Adapt it for your own purposes to help you create balance in your financial life. Having this system in place practically guarantees slow, consistent growth. The percentages stay constant, but the numbers will likely increase from year to year as you grow and as your business grows. Train yourself to live within the boundaries of this system if you intend to be financially free.

To begin, if you are self-employed, take 30 percent of your total earnings out for taxes and set it aside. The remaining balance will count as your 100 percent.

- **60 percent:** Lifestyle account—This account represents your necessities and lifestyle. It includes house payments, groceries, medical checkups and everything in between.

- **10 percent:** Wealth creation account—This account includes investments, IRAs, mutual funds, stocks and bonds and real estate. Once money goes into this account, you never touch it. You can take out the interest you earn on investments, or you can leave it alone and let it grow to the point where you eventually live off the interest you earn every month.

- **5 percent:** Joy account—This is the money you use to play. You may not think you can afford this, but once you actually allocate a number to fun, it feels (and is) less impulsive and you'll feel less guilty.

- **10 percent:** Dream account—This is the account you use when you save for big-ticket items, such as vacations, a new car, a dream home or new furniture. Saving is a habit that will help you to maintain your money management system.

- **5 percent:** Enlightenment account—This account is for educating and enriching yourself, taking classes or hiring a coach in whatever area you need or want, whether it's business or personal growth. How do expect to grow your business if you don't grow?

- **10 percent:** Spiritual growth account—This account is for tithing. Peleg believes that giving back with joy, gratitude and non-attachment, and expecting nothing in return acknowledges the spiritual source that is within the universe.

CASH FLOW VS. PROFITABILITY

BY DAVID BAKER, RECOURSES, INC.

The first step toward an improved business environment is stepping out of denial with a deep sigh of relief. You will begin to use newfound energy to fix the problems instead of mask them. We all have ways of talking about specific situations that make them a bit more palatable.

DISTINGUISHING BETWEEN CASH AND PROFIT

One example we see frequently goes like this: "We've been having some cash flow difficulty." By definition, cash flow difficulties are rare. If your cash flow difficulties are recurring, what you really are struggling with is profitability, not cash flow. That's a very important distinction.

Very profitable firms can have an occasional bout with cash flow disease. For instance, a client might withhold payment on a large bill, a major project might have to be scrapped or a key person might leave the firm.

On the other hand, firms that consistently struggle with cash flow cannot be profitable in any real sense. But we talk about "cash flow difficulties" because that phrasing makes it seem like we are being tossed by the vagaries of the marketplace, as if somehow this is a problem that is out of our control.

And there seems to be little connection between volume of work and cash flow struggles. Some of the clients we help are terribly busy but still not profitable. Those are often the firms that have misunderstood marketing (marketing is about control, not growth).

STARTING WITH CANDOR

Why is this important? Back to the original point: Unless you admit that the core problem is profitability, you'll make unwise decisions about cash flow. That might mean incurring fixed obligations when you can't afford them just to get out of the immediate crunch (e.g., credit line abuse or leases for depreciating assets).

Here's a suggestion: Don't manage your business based on cash in the bank. It's important to have it (at least two month's worth of overhead), but it's an indicator far too close to the events at hand to provide any meaningful information on the health of your business. Think of measuring cash as measuring how hungry you are at any given moment. One cheeseburger will fix it, at least temporarily.

And don't pay too much attention to your income statement, either. It's a much better indicator of your health (if it's on an accrual basis), but it still gives you information about recent, short periods of data. And it doesn't fully account for what you do with the money once you get it. Think of measuring profitability as getting on the scale to check your weight. If you had a supersized drink with that cheeseburger, you are going to weigh two pounds extra, whether it was water or 250 calories of drippy, sweet cola.

The slowest moving—and most accurate—method of measuring your health is to look at your balance sheet. Like nothing else, this accounts for nearly all of the decisions you've made. More specifically, compare your equity (assets minus liabilities) every quarter and chart it for comparison purposes. Look at the direction of movement, not the speed of movement. Think of this as measuring your body fat or taking a treadmill test. One cheeseburger won't affect it, but a bunch of them will.

TAKING THE NEXT STEP

So you've read this far and buy the argument. You are busy, your clients love what you do for them, but you're ready to join Cash-flow-ers Anonymous and admit that the problem is deeper. Don't you dare reach for that "raise our hourly rate" button! If you want to position yourself higher in the marketplace, raise your rates. But that's another subject.

> If you want to make more money, though, quit subsidizing clients and start charging what it really takes to get the job done. Until you fix that, you'll be forever plagued with a problem that should be rare.
>
> And start by admitting that you have a significant profitability issue.
>

Now it's time to start learning about the numbers that matter to your business. Make a commitment to yourself right now to make this change, to get "good with numbers." Otherwise, you'll be building a house on a foundation of sand and, sooner or later, things will start to slip.

CHAPTER 8
WHAT SHOULD I CHARGE?

Designers spend an inordinate and disproportionate amount of time determining pricing and fretting over it. But there is no right or wrong answer when it comes to pricing. It's all completely subjective and dependent on a wide variety of factors.

Cameron Foote of Creative Business defines "getting pricing right" as "charging enough to ensure good profitability, but not so much as to lose a client to competition."

In this chapter, we'll cover the nuts and bolts of estimating a project and figuring out how much to charge.

UNDERSTANDING WHAT YOU ARE SELLING

One major obstacle for many designers is the belief that what you charge is related to your value as a person. Wrong!

First of all, it's not about you. A prospect or client will often ask, "How much do you charge for a web site?" or "How much do you charge for a logo?" or "How much do you charge for a fill-in-the-blank?" as if they are buying a can of tomatoes.

Look at the way that question is constructed: "How much do you charge for ..."

If you were selling tennis shoes, and somebody said, "How much do you charge for tennis shoes?" you wouldn't say, "I charge $100 for tennis shoes." You would say, "Tennis shoes cost $100."

It's the same with design services. It has nothing to do with what "you charge." It's not about you, and it never will be. Shift your mindset to think instead about what the product and the process costs. When someone says, "How much do you charge for a web site?" take the "you" out of it and respond with, "A web site can cost $X."

You're Not Selling Your Time

Time flies when you're doing your creative work, especially on the projects you really enjoy. In fact, you may not notice how much time you're spending. Some designers don't realize they've spent much more time than they had initially allowed for. They don't dare divide the number of hours by their hourly rate, only to discover they're making little more than minimum wage. That's a rude awakening. And it's all the more reason to track your time.

It's a cliché, but it's true: Time is money. The more time one project takes, the less time you have for another, and the less money you make.

Many designers price by the hour, and for all the wrong reasons.

First of all, it's easy to price your services by the hour. It's clean, it's orderly and it doesn't require much math. But it is not to your benefit, especially in the long run.

This is because the faster you are and the better you get, the more money you will make. A logo might take you five hours today when, two years ago, it may have taken twenty. You get better—sometimes a lot better—with time. But if you charge by the hour, as you get better, you earn less. Does that make sense?

Also, design is a creative process. Not only is there no rule about how long it should take; there is a certain amount of inspiration involved. You probably don't know how long it will take for your best ideas to come. They could come right away, or they could take a while. Should you be paid based on how long it takes for your ideas to come together? Is that how you should determine how much money you earn?

What you are selling is your years of experience, the effort you've expended developing your skills and talents, and your resulting expertise.

What you are selling is peace of mind. Not many clients understand design, so they don't know what they're buying, and they know they don't know. So it's your job to make them comfortable and safe in the knowledge that you do understand and will take care of everything. If you do that, the good clients will choose you, even if you're the highest bidder.

What you are selling is your brain, your attention and your creative imagination applied to a client's specific problem, and that has a value. It's not an objective value; in fact, it's highly subjective, which makes it challenging to quantify. That's why it's easier to charge by the hour.

That value—your price—is based on several factors, including geographic location, timing, what the market will bear, the urgency of your prospect's need, aggravation factor (or lack thereof), what it's worth to you to do it, and your level of desperation (hopefully low to nonexistent), just to name a few.

Your responsibility in estimating each job is to determine what that value is for each project. Once you have made that determination, through a series of steps we will explore in this chapter, you present that to the prospect for their feedback. Then, through conversation, you either come to an agreement about the value of your services, or you don't. It's that simple.

The Value of Your Work

There is no intrinsic value to your work. Its value is based on perceptions. The perceived value of any project comes as a result of positioning your services properly through your marketing and sales process. You have to understand your client well to know what she will find valuable. Maybe she cares most how well the project is executed. Or that you meet all the deadlines. Or that you deliver quality that exceeds her expectations. Is your client looking for quality, ease, time saved, lack of stress? Once you know what's important to each of your clients, you can position yourself to provide exactly that. And they will pay for it.

Value comes with service, not design. Design has become a commodity. Your clients can get it anywhere. They can do it themselves. (How many times have you heard a client say they just got Photoshop?) Your competitors are up and down the pricing spectrum. There will always be someone whose price is lower, so you must understand what value you add, and use that to position your services.

Customer service will make you stand apart. You add value by anticipating needs, by under-promising and over-delivering. That's why they appreciate it when you take the lead. They want you to be in charge so they can focus on other things. That's how you sell peace of mind through design.

THE IMPORTANCE OF AN HOURLY RATE

In order to run a healthy and profitable business, you must know how long it takes you to do various tasks and projects; in essence, you must know your expenses, and time is a major expense. If you're just starting out in business, you'll probably be guessing at first, and you'll make lots of mistakes—that's the good news.

You should be tracking your time and that of any freelancer or employee who works for you.

If you've been at this for a while, your timesheets or time-tracking software will give you detailed reports of what you spend on each project.

Your hourly rate is not your price, though. It's one of the building blocks of your price, so you need to know what it is. Your time is what you track, and it should be the basis of your pricing, though only for internal purposes. In other words, use your hourly rate to determine what to charge for a project, but never reveal that hourly rate in a proposal or in conversations with your client. Not only is it none of their business, it also wouldn't mean anything to them. An hourly rate is only relevant in relation to how long a project takes, and they have no idea how long design takes. You open the door to their assumptions by talking about your hourly rate.

So when a client asks you how long a project will take, never say, "This will take X hours." The only thing they need to know about time is when they can expect to receive the deliverable.

Instead, you say, "Let me check what we have on the schedule, and I'll get back to you with a time frame. In the meantime, let me know your deadline and I will do my best to accommodate it."

Salary and Overhead

Once you have an accurate hourly rate, it should be used as the basis for your project fees—again, though, only for internal purposes.

At the end of the day, you have to know how much you must charge, which is different from how much you should charge. What you should charge is up to you and takes into consideration how much others charge for the same services—what's competitive and what's not.

In addition to your design and production fees, there are other elements of a project that must be factored into the price. Your salary and overheard are two crucial components.

Many creative, self-employed people do not include their salaries in the overhead; they see their salaries as the profit they take out of the business. But salaries are a business expense. Profit comes after all expenses are paid, including all salaries. The rule is to pay yourself first.

To determine a number for your salary, ask yourself how much you want to make in a year, realistically. Set attainable goals, and keep raising the bar. That's how you get to six figures or a million or whatever your dream number is.

Also included in your overhead are all the expenses required to keep the doors open. It's the cost of doing business, including your computer, the monthly phone bill, insurance, maintenance, supplies and computer software. Some are fixed expenses that don't fluctuate from month to month; others depend entirely on usage, which you can control.

YOUR BUSINESS OVERHEAD

Month:	
Year:	

AUTOMOBILE
Fuel:
Insurance and registration:
Car payment/lease:
Parking:
Repairs and maintenance:
Subtotal:

INSURANCE
Health and dental:
Liability:
Worker's comp:
Subtotal:

OFFICE EXPENSES
Internet access:
Licenses:
Business phone and fax:
Mobile phone:
Web hosting and e-mail:
Rent:
Utilities:
Supplies:
Computers:
Software:
Subtotal:

TRAVEL
Hotels:
Airfare:
Rental cars:

Subtotal:

MARKETING

E-mail marketing service:

Postage:

Printing:

Client dining:

Client gifts:

Copywriting:

Subtotal:

PROFESSIONAL FEES

Accounting:

Lawyer/legal fees:

Bookkeeping:

Subtotal:

EMPLOYEES
Salaries:
Medical benefits:
Taxes:
Other employee costs:
Subtotal:

OTHER EXPENSES
Subtotal:

TOTAL OVERHEAD

What Will Your Profit Be?

Once you know your overhead, the next question is: How much profit do you want to earn? Ten percent? Twenty percent? Your profit is not tied to how much time the project takes; it is built into your hourly rate. If, however, once you have estimated for a potential project, the number you come up with feels too low, or if the client's budget allows for more, you are free to add additional profit. Again, you're in business, among other things, to make money.

According to *Creative Business*, "Profit is a business necessity, not a luxury. Among other things, profit allows a firm to fund a reserve against times of slow business, to provide for future capital requirements, and to give principals compensation beyond their salaries as a return for investment risk."

How to Figure Your Hourly Rate

Most designers wonder if they're charging enough. You probably do, too. And you probably aren't.

Where does your hourly rate come from? Out of thin air? From an industry guide? Is it a number that's close to or the same as what your competition charges? Is it a number you chose because it's comfortable to you and no one complains about it? (By the way, if you're getting every job you bid on, you're probably not charging enough.)

Or did you sit down and figure out how much you need to charge in order to earn the living you need and achieve your goals?

For most people, the answer to that last question is no. But if you don't figure out what your hourly rate must be in order to cover your expenses, how will you know if you are charging enough?

Here's the process you must go through to figure out the hourly rate that you must charge in order to earn the living you want. Follow along with the example that starts on page 183.

Step 1: Determine your salary. That's right, you get to decide. What is the salary you need your business to pay you, before taxes? Let's work with $40,000. This is the "100 percent" figure that corresponds to Peleg Top's Personal Money Management System (see page 168).

Add 30 percent on top of that to cover your income tax. Thirty percent of $40,000 is $12,000. Therefore, you need to pull $52,000 per year from your business in order to get your desired salary.

Step 2: Figure your labor hourly rate. That is how much money you make for every hour that you work, or, more accurately, for every hour that you bill a client. To do that, determine how many hours you'll be working for clients in a year. 1,142 hours is an industry standard used for figuring hourly rates, and it's based on a 40-hour work week. (If you're working part-time, figure it based on the number of hours you actually work per week.)

Based on a standard 40-hour work week, there are 2,080 working hours in a year (52 weeks x 40 hours per week). In reality, however, people get sick and take days off. The standard number used for days off is 176 hours (that's 22 eight-hour days). So, 2,080 – 76 = 1,904 working hours in the year.

That doesn't meaning you're billing all 1,904 hours. If your business is healthy and thriving, you'll spend approximately 40 percent of your time on administrative duties, managing, invoicing, filing, marketing, travel, and so forth. That means 60 percent of your time is billable. Sixty percent of 1,904 is 1,142.

To calculate your hourly rate, take the total salary you need ($52,000) and divide it by 1,142 hours. That brings your labor hourly rate to $45.53. If you work and bill 1,142 hours at this rate, you'll make the after-tax income of $40,000 you want.

Step 3: Determine your business overhead by adding up all your expenses. (See Business Overhead Worksheet on page 179.) It's very important that you understand how much it costs to run your business. A lot of people, especially solo entrepreneurs, underestimate this. If you work from home, your home and business expenses probably get mixed together. Plus, working from home, you don't "feel" the expenses as much as you would if you worked in an office and had to write separate checks for things such as rent, phone and Internet. That's why it's important to separate the two. You should have a business checking account and understand what percentage of your home expenses actually are business expenses. If you had to go out tomorrow and rent an office and not use the convenience of home, how much would that cost?

In our example, let's say you spend $35,000 per year to run your business. So add $35,000 to your salary ($52,000) and you get a total of $87,000. That's how much you must bring in to cover your salary and overhead.

If you are spending $35,000 a year on a business that's paying you only $40,000, your business expenses are really high and you should look for places to cut expenses.

Step 4: Make sure your hourly rate covers your overhead. Your overhead hourly rate is what you must charge just to cover your overhead. You determine this by first figuring what percentage of your total salary is the business overhead. So take the overhead ($35,000) and divide it by the total salary ($52,000), which in our example is 67.3 percent. That's your overhead hourly rate.

Multiply that percentage (67.3 percent) by your labor hourly rate ($45.53) to find out how much to add to cover not only your salary, but also your expenses. In this example, $30.64 an hour will cover overhead.

Step 5: Add your labor hourly rate to your overhead hourly rate to find the total hourly rate required to cover both your salary and your overhead. So: $45.53 + $30.64 = $76.17.

Step 6: Add your profit. You're working to make a profit, right? It's up to you how much profit you want to make. Ten to twenty percent is standard. In this example, we'll add a 10 percent profit. So 10 percent of the combined hourly rate ($76.17), which is $7.62. Add that to the combined labor and overhead rate to get $83.79. Round it up to $85 an hour.

So your business is thriving, and if you're billing 1,142 hours at $85 per hour, after business expenses and taxes, you will take home the $40,000 that you want, plus a 10 percent profit.

Now, $85 is the base hourly rate to work with. It's not necessarily what you should be charging; it's the minimum you must charge to run this business profitably. Once you calculate this rate for yourself, you'll know the base of how much you'll have to figure into a project. You must charge *at least* this much. You can charge more—as much more as you like.

If you're figuring out an hourly rate for a two-person studio, you simply double the 1,142 hours since you have two people working. So 1,142 hours becomes 2,284 hours. Since the salary has to be doubled, the available hours have to be doubled. But there should be only one business overhead number because it's the overhead for the whole business.

YOUR HOURLY RATE

STEP 1

A. Estimated salary

> ex: $40,000
> yours:

B. Estimated taxes (add 30%)

> ex: $12,000
> yours:

C. Total salary for the year

> ex: $52,000
> yours:

D. Yearly business hours

> ex: 2,080, or 1,904 after vacation and sick days
> yours:

E. 60% billable efficiency

> ex: 1,142 billable hours per year
> yours:

STEP 2

F. Labor hourly rate: total salary ÷ billable hours (line C ÷ line E)

ex: $45.53
yours:

STEP 3

G. Business overhead expenses

ex: $35,000
yours:

H. Business overhead + salary (line C + line G)

ex: $87,000
yours:

STEP 4

J. Overhead as % of salary (line G ÷ line C)

ex: 67.3%
yours:

STEP 5

K. Overhead hourly rate: labor hourly rate x overhead % (line F x line J)

ex: $30.64
yours:

L. Rate to recover income + overhead: (line F + line K)

ex: $76.17
yours:

This is what you must charge; now add your profit.

STEP 6

M. Profit percentage: hourly rate x 10%

> ex: $7.62
> yours:

N. Add that to your hourly rate

> ex: $83.79
> yours:

This is what you should charge per hour. Then, round it up:

> ex: $85.00
> yours:

Other Factors to Consider When Pricing a Project

Project management

Every job will involve some level of project management, and it will differ according to the complexity of the project. Designing a logo will generally require the involvement of fewer people than producing a magazine or an annual report. That's why you must charge extra for project management. Don't give away your time; build it into the final number. Add a percentage of hours that you think it will take to manage the project. That percentage comes from your experience and your tracking, but if you have don't have much of either one, start with 25 percent to be safe, then keep track and see if that's accurate.

Studio rate/production

Use the hourly rate worksheet to derive your studio hourly rate—what it costs to keep your studio open every day—which may be different from your labor hourly rate. Use your studio hourly rate for estimating purposes only. Don't have different hourly rates for different phases of projects.

Revisions

The ideal job may be one where you present your concepts and the client loves them. They choose one (your favorite), you execute it, they still love it and you create final art. Alas, this doesn't happen often, which is why you must allow for revisions in your estimate. But how many rounds of revisions should you allow for? This is another mystery, especially when working with new clients.

One thing is for sure: The more people involved, the more rounds of revisions there will be. In fact, large corporate clients and big projects are likely to have many rounds of revisions. Exactly how many is hard to say. Your clients will know better than you. So before you present your pricing, ask about their approval process. Ask how many rounds of revisions they realistically need. If they tell you they need eight rounds, then that's what you estimate for. There is no right number of revisions. You can have as many rounds of revisions as you or they want. But it must be factored into the price.

Anything above the agreed number of revisions is charged at your "revision hourly rate." This is yet another hourly rate. It should be no less than the studio hourly rate and probably a bit higher.

It could also be very high—as high as $300 an hour—because it should convey this message: "We don't want to do revisions."

Do your best to avoid several unexpected rounds of revisions. They are problematic for everyone involved. If you tell your client early on what the revision hourly rate is, they are likely to avoid most revisions and sign off sooner rather than later.

Markup

Markup is an amount added by a seller (you) to the cost of a commodity to cover expenses and profit in fixing the selling price. It's like a broker fee that you take for facilitating a process. It is standard business practice to add a markup on anything that you have to oversee and coordinate, including printing, mailing lists, fulfillment and copywriting.

Some designers feel insecure about charging a markup. You may feel it's deceptive, that you don't deserve it. Forget all that. You're not stealing or gouging your clients. You're not "getting away" with anything. At the grocery store, you can be sure you're not paying what the grocer paid. Standard markup at retail is often 100 percent or more. Every time something goes through another pair of hands, a layer of fees is added. This is business, and your clients understand and probably even expect it.

You needn't disclose your markup in any way that calls extra attention to it. It's built in to your pricing and will likely not be questioned. And if, on occasion, a client resists paying a markup, you can offer to let them take care of that aspect of the project on their own, whether it's printing or something else.

Standard markup in the design industry is 10–30 percent, depending on several factors, including who the client is, the size of the company, where you are located and what they would pay for the services or products if they procured them directly.

Rush charges

Clients can have a rush job for a variety of reasons, such as a shift in priorities or an opportunity that arises out of the blue. But often, it's due to a lack of planning. The project was sitting on their desks for six weeks before it rose to the top of the pile. If you don't charge rush fees, you will pay the price for their lack of planning.

Standard rush charges start at 50 percent, but it can sometimes go as high as 100 percent. The rule is that the less time you have to work, the higher the percentage you charge for the rush.

Clients know rush means more money, whether they acknowledge it or not. This can be a fuzzy area because there is no standard for what constitutes a rush. That's why you need to establish what your normal pace is and what a rush is. You also need to let your clients know from the moment they say, "I need this yesterday," this situation qualifies as a rush. In fact, make a description of this process accessible to clients; you can even publish it on your web site.

Rushing generally adds chaos to a project, so everything you can do to bring order will eliminate potential for miscommunication, or worse. When a client is in a hurry, the estimating process often gets shortened, sometimes even skipped over altogether in the interest of time. But this is not in anyone's best interest, including your client's.

Take the time to go through your regular process; simply speed it up due to the circumstances. Always provide a written estimate, even it's an abbreviated one, and insist that your client sign off on it before beginning the work. Sometimes an e-mail agreement is enough, especially for a current client. Whatever the medium, simply say, "I'm sending you the agreement today, and I will need your approval and a deposit before we start the work." Don't forgo the deposit. They may have reasons why they can't get the deposit to you quickly. Consider this a red flag and don't back down. Simply ask, "What can we do to secure this project?" Offering the option to pay by credit card could speed things along.

Be happy to get a rush job because rush jobs are very lucrative, especially if you are well organized. In fact, you can position your services with a focus on quick turnaround, and people will pay extra for it. That in itself could set you apart from the crowd.

If you don't want to do rush jobs, then you must train your clients to think and plan ahead. When you have clients whose projects are seasonal or regular, don't wait for them to initiate the process. Be proactive, create a schedule and keep them on track. Let them know with plenty of advance warning that they'll pay rush charges if they don't get started soon. Stay on top of it, and take the lead.

Volume discount

In some industries, it is customary to offer a discount to clients who do a lot of business—in essence, an incentive whereby the more they buy, the less they pay. This makes sense for printed or manufactured goods because it costs less to make more. But that isn't usually the case with design. More work requires more time.

Sometimes, however, there is a savings and you are free to pass it along to your client. For example, if they have three related projects, such as a rebranding, a web site and a printed brochure based on the new branding, you can offer it a la carte or as a package deal. "If you sign off on all three right now, we'll take X percent off the total." Sometimes this helps in the selling process. Plus, it helps your cash flow, too.

If you do decide to offer this, make the offer when you first present the proposal, not in response to a pricing objection further along in the process.

SIX STRATEGIES FOR MANAGING CASH FLOW

1. Keep your overhead as low as possible. Eighty percent of overhead is salary, and the rest is maintenance: running the business and marketing. Keep your expenses as low as possible, even during flush periods.

2. Keep two to four months of overhead in a savings account for rainy days. Not only will it be important for practical reasons, it also will give you peace of mind. Don't touch that money unless you really have to. Tapping into that account should be a red flag that the business is not generating enough cash flow to cover your expenses. It could be your billing, your marketing or your flow of prospects. That's the time to find out what's wrong.

3. Open a business line of credit. It's like having a business credit card that you draw money against, but it's a larger amount of money, usually $25,000 or more. It generally costs $100–$200 a year to keep this type of account open, but it's worth it because it will be there in case you need extra funds to cover yourself for a couple of months.

4. Become a merchant and take credit cards for payment on jobs. You pay a small percentage per transaction for the convenience (which

you can also bill to the client), but the benefits outweigh the tiny cost. It puts money in your pocket right away. You do the job, and you get paid the same week. And you'd be surprised how many clients will appreciate being able to use their credit cards, including corporate clients with corporate credit cards. They like it because they usually get benefits, such as frequent flyer mileage points.

5. Negotiate with your vendors. As you develop strong relationships with your vendors you can negotiate better payment terms. Why would they give you better terms? Because you are loyal to them and you give them a lot of business. Instead of the usual thirty days, ask for sixty or ninety days. Every little bit helps. Then, when you do pay them, use a credit card, which gives you another thirty days.

6. Put deposits in escrow. In order to avoid a situation whereby you get paid upfront and then spend the money before the actual bills come in, put that money in an escrow account so you don't spend it, and so it can earn interest until you have to pay the vendor.

Bookkeeping and Tracking Expenses

There are tools you can use to facilitate this process. QuickBooks and MYOB are two popular accounting software programs for small businesses that allow you to track your expenses and bill your clients. These programs may appear to be complicated to a creative mind like yours, but they're not. They just take some time and instruction if you are going to do it yourself. It's well worth the investment of time to learn QuickBooks, whether you teach yourself or hire a bookkeeper to get you set up.

Once you have all the information in place and up to date, you can create any kind of report you need any time of day. You can look at your profit and loss, your bank balance, what you're spending with a certain vendor, how much a particular client has been worth year to year, and which clients are more than thirty days late in their payment so you can make a few collection calls instead of being hit with a cash flow crunch down the road.

If you don't have the time or the knowledge to invest in this essential aspect of your business, don't let it go. Hire a bookkeeper to come in and do it for you for three or four hours a week. It's a perfect solution for a small business. The bookkeeper does data entry, payroll, bill-paying and reconciling the bank statements. He can even do your billing for you.

And if you are doing your invoices in QuarkXPress because they look pretty, it's time to get more professional about it. The look of your invoices is irrelevant to your clients. In fact, you may even get paid more quickly when they come out of accounting software looking like a real invoice.

HIRE SUBCONTRACTORS

You can't do everything yourself. If you try to, your business will remain very small, and the tasks you don't get to will either go undone or be done below par. That's why one reality of being self-employed is that you need to identify your strengths, and then get help with your weaknesses. Even if you want your business to be small, recognize that it is limiting, too.

One way to get help is to hire freelancers. In fact, it's smart to have a pool of resources available and on call when you need them, so you don't have to go searching in your moment of need and make a quick decision without enough information.

Most freelancers work on an hourly rate. They can come to your office, or they can work in their own spaces. You can decide which makes the most sense for your needs. But when it comes to paying freelancers, pay project fees rather than hourly rates, whenever possible. This is for the same reasons you should be charging projects fees rather than an hourly rate: You hire them for their talent and their output, not how much time they spend. When you have a budget from a client, you can't simply give a subcontractor a blank slate.

HOW TO RAISE YOUR PRICES

BY DAVID BAKER

Every year or two, creative service firms begin thinking about their pricing, and specifically whether to raise it and how to go about it. Here are a few thoughts for you to consider.

THREE PLACES TO START

First, don't think of your hourly rate as a pricing tool, because it's really more of a positioning tool. It is just one of many inputs that feed how prospects and clients view your services, but it is a substantive one. How much you charge per hour is directly related to the perceived value of your services. In fact, the only time you should talk about your hourly rate is when you want to make a positioning statement or in answer to a direct question asked by a prospect or client. Otherwise, don't talk about it.

Second, don't think of your hourly rate as a way to make money, because making money is more about utilization than pricing. To expand on this, there is absolutely no correlation between a firm's hourly rate and how much money they make, but there is a very direct correlation between how many hours they get paid for versus how many hours they spend on any given body of work. The latter distinction is about utilization, or what we call "billable efficiency." If a given firm is not making enough money, they often are tempted first to raise their hourly rate, but that's going straight to second base without first rounding first base. First base is making sure that you're capturing all your time properly, no matter at what hourly rate you're billing it. Keep these issues separate, and fix your utilization first. If you've fixed that and still want to make more money, or if your current hourly rate is too low from a positioning standpoint, then think about raising your hourly rate.

Third, concentrate on being consultative rather than getting trapped in a transactional mentality. One example of this might be thinking in terms of hours in the first place. Sure, some of you are on open billing or retainers, but you're really trapped if you're billing by the hour. You can make a fair amount of money that way, but you can make more if you simply set a price that the client accepts or rejects. If they accept it, you then work on getting it done by spending a number of hours that is equal to or less than the hours you estimated it would require. This usually requires a particular, focused expertise, which in turn allows for a process of solving client problems that is defined and proprietary.

Having embraced these points, suppose you want to adjust your hourly rate. Here are some suggestions on how to do it.

SIX THOUGHTS ABOUT HOW TO RAISE YOUR PRICES

First, don't change it every year. Doing so is transactional, as if the rate of inflation is built into your hourly rate. It is not, and thinking that way will make you look more like a seller of commodities than of advisory services. So look at it every year, but change it every three to five years.

Second, change it by a significant amount or don't bother (assuming that you don't have a lot of catching up to do in the first place). That means you'll increase it typically by ten to thirty dollars per hour, or it's not worth the disruption.

Third, if that disruption would endanger some of your client relationships, just do it for prospects (i.e., new clients). There's only so much compromise that's prudent when trying to keep "legacy" clients happy, but sometimes it's a short-term solution you're willing to entertain as you bite your tongue and live with it until you have better choices. (Remember that client turnover, if it's for the right reasons, is always your friend.)

Fourth, tell those who need to know a couple of months in advance, and then say no more about it when the time comes.

Fifth, position the price increase as an inevitable outcome from a careful look at your profitability targets. In other words, do an internal study that leads to (surprising) findings that virtually requires you to raise your rates to meet those targets. Make it a considered move and not some gut reaction, and then blame the study that you wish you could argue with but cannot.

Sixth, try to provide choices to individual clients. Above all, that's what clients want. Even choosing between two bad options gives them the sense of control, which every client craves. There is no

RULES FOR DOING PRO BONO WORK

Nonprofit does not mean "no profit." Nonprofits are still running a business, it's just that at the end of the year, when they close their books, if there is a profit, it ideally goes back into the services they provide instead of being distributed among shareholders or owners.

Nonprofit does not always mean they're looking for pro bono, either. A healthy nonprofit will budget for marketing and design like any other business. In fact, some nonprofits have big marketing budgets because they know the value of marketing. It's a line item in their budget—and that includes hiring design firms.

Smaller nonprofits ($2 million or less operating budget), however, of which there are hundreds of thousands all over the country, are usually looking for pro bono work. If you want to work with nonprofits, it's better for your business to look for bigger nonprofits that have marketing budgets to work with.

Here are some guidelines to follow if you want to work with nonprofits or do pro bono work:

- Believe in the cause. Jeff Fisher, author of *The Savvy Designer's Guide to Success*, knows that to do his best work, he must have a passion for the cause: "With the large number of requests I received for pro bono work, I also realized I needed to create some personal guidelines in regard to donated time. I now only consider donating my services if the project is related to education, nonprofit performing arts groups, children's causes or issues in which I have a strong personal interest. I will also only take on a limited number of pro bono projects in any one calendar year."

- Make it a fair exchange. Pro bono work is not "free" work. You're giving something of value to the organization, and you are getting something in return. You may be doing it for a warm, fuzzy feeling. You may be doing it for exposure. Whatever your reason, be clear about it because, unfortunately, the IRS does not recognize work that is done pro bono, so there is no tax benefit. The IRS states: "Although you cannot deduct the value of your time or services, you can deduct the expenses you incur while donating your services to a qualified organization."

- Maintain your standard process. Don't let your standard process fall by the wayside just because no money is changing hands. Your contract will be even more important in this type of situation. As you would with any other client, adhere to your schedule and the acceptable number of revisions.

- Make sure they have a budget to produce what you design. You don't want to find out in the middle of the process that they only have $500 to print the annual report you designed. That's a waste of your time and resources. Bring this up in the early stages of the process and, if you find out they don't have enough of a production budget, offer different options for production.

- Ask for creative latitude. One of the reasons to do pro bono work is to create work for your portfolio, so be sure to negotiate for the opportunity to use more creative flexibility in the project.

- Get paid if the work is not used. What if the event for which you're designing an invitation is canceled at the last minute? Does your work simply disappear, and are your efforts for naught? Be sure to stipulate in your contract what happens if the work is not used, whether it be a payment to you or something else.

- Present your work to the board of directors. One good reason to do pro bono work is for exposure and connections with people in important places. Before you agree to anything, negotiate to present your work, perhaps in its final form, to the board of directors of the nonprofit. In fact, you should insist on this. These boards often are made up of civic-minded business people who travel in very different business and social circles from you. And they are generally very good networkers. It's essential that you meet them in person (rather than be offered the chance to follow up with them later) to make that personal connection.

- Get a design credit. Negotiate for an actual credit on the work, whether it's printed or electronic. In both cases, a web address is the best credit you can get because it not only tells the name of your firm, it also directs new prospects to your web site, where they can learn more about your services.

- Ask for samples. One main reason to do pro bono work is to be able to show it off, which you can't do unless you have plenty of samples. So ask for at least a hundred samples, and then use them in your promotional efforts. You can easily do a separately targeted mailing built around this one piece at very little marketing expense.

- Get mentioned in their press release. Often, a nonprofit will take advantage of free publicity and will send out a press release related to the project, especially if it's a high-end job for an event. Ask to be included in the media coverage. All you need is one or two lines to describe your involvement, which, when posted online, will be good for your search engine rankings as well.

- Set boundaries. Know when it's done. These projects can go on forever, especially when there are no payment terms. Be strict about what you give and what they get. It will protect you in the end.

These rules can also apply to working with family and friends. Remember to keep the process as professional as possible in order to avoid potential miscommunication or unrealistic expectations.

SHOULD I BARTER AND TRADE?

Depending on your business goals and cash flow, you may be able to negotiate less common, but sometimes viable, alternative arrangements. Although it's less popular, bartering can be an acceptable alternative for a cash-starved client offering an exciting creative opportunity.

First, check with your accountant, because barter arrangements may be taxable. When bartering, make sure you negotiate, in writing, an equal value exchange. For pro bono and nonprofit work, or for projects you accept at a reduced rate, you also can ask for full creative control and compensation for all out-of-pocket expenses. The downside is that you risk establishing a reputation for these types of arrangements, possibly lessening the perceived value of your services. If you decide to negotiate such nontraditional agreements, treat them like your other professional relationships and have them approved, in writing, by the client. Also, always emphasize that you're proposing a nontraditional, one-time agreement that may not be applicable for the next project.

Now that you have clarified your own policies about the way you handle money in your business, it's time to talk about those policies with your clients.

CHAPTER 9
HOW DO I TALK ABOUT MONEY?

Now that you've dealt with your own issues—you've figured out how to manage your money, how to think about pricing and how much to charge—it's time to take this information out into the world and start talking to prospects and clients about it.

Here's the reality: We live in a capitalist society. You are in business, and you can't do business without dealing with money. If you try, you're likely to get yourself in trouble.

Your prospects are considering hiring you as a professional. They don't expect you work for free. They have a budget (whether they reveal it or not) and they expect to negotiate with you about your fees. In fact, if you don't take the initiative and bring up the topic of money, the impression you leave is that of an amateur, and, as a result, they may not take you seriously.

IT'S OKAY TO TALK ABOUT MONEY

Talking about money doesn't have to be distasteful or confrontational. In fact, it is one of the clearest planes on which to speak because there are no blurry lines when it comes to numbers. They either add up or they don't. Your prospects either have the money or they don't. It's your choice whether to make a big drama out of it. We suggest you don't.

Smart (i.e., desirable) clients know how much things cost. This is the type of client you should be looking for. Talking about money will not be difficult for them, and they will make the process easy for you because they are:

- accustomed to spending money on design;
- familiar with budgets; and
- spending their company's money, not their own personal money

Step 1: Weed out inappropriate prospects.

First, take these steps to qualify your prospects to determine whether they're "smart" clients. You need to develop and know your own criteria for whom you'll work with and whom you won't. Here are some factors to consider and questions to ask yourself:

- **The client.** How closely does the client fit the profile of your ideal client? Is there potential for future work, or is this a one-time project? How does this fit with your long-term goals?

- **The project.** Is it a project you're interested in? Will it allow you to learn anything new? How does it compare with other projects you've done? Is anything about the project in line with the future direction of your work? Or is it more in line with where you've already been? If it's a small project, can it serve as an introduction and get you in the door with a client who is likely to have more work later on?

- **The fee.** Does this project meet your minimum fee? It's important to know the minimum fee for which you will pick up a pen or open a new document. Find this number using your hourly rate and what you know about how much administrative time is involved to begin a project, manage it and bill for it. You may come up with $500 or $2,500, and it may depend on the current state of your business. But it's essential to know your minimum.

- **The people.** Do you like the people involved? Do they have experience working with and hiring outsiders? Do they seem easy to work with? Do they display clear communication skills (verbal and written)? Do they spend hours talking? Will you have to accommodate for any of these characteristics by scheduling more meetings? Will you need to add an "aggravation factor" into your fee?

- **Work style.** What is the office environment? Are they punctual? Are they organized? Better to find out now rather than later that they are disorganized, which often creates a chaotic process no matter how much order you try to instill.

You can find the answers to all of these questions in an initial phone call and decide quickly whether to pursue each prospect.

Rules and policies are important to have, but you must also know when to make an exception. If your plate is empty, you might be tempted to take on a small project that is below your minimum. Consider devoting that time to marketing instead; it's usually a better investment in the long run.

USE THE WEB TO WEED OUT TIRE-KICKERS

There may be prospects who aren't even worth the initial phone call, so you need a way to filter them out without wasting your time. Your web site can serve as that filter.

Post a form on your web site that prospects fill out if they want a proposal. The serious prospects will take the time to fill out your form. Tire-kickers and those shopping for prices will not.

The form, once filled out, also will give structure to the request, help to focus your potential client and put in one place all (or most) of the information you need to get started preparing a proposal.

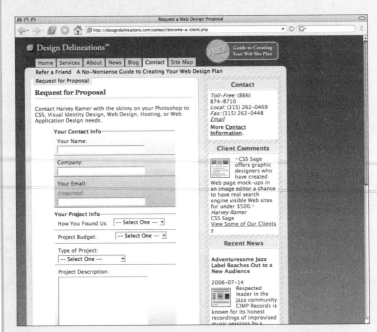

Here is the proposal request form from http://designdelineations.com.

Beyond that, this structure also gives your prospect a sense of how you work and some of the requirements of working with you. It's part of your positioning as a professional.

Here are some of the questions you should include on your web site's proposal request form:

- How did you hear about us?
- Briefly describe your company.
- What is your immediate need?
- Do you have a budget?
- What is your deadline?
- How and when is it best to contact you?

The downside of this form is that it can be a deterrent to serious prospects who are in a hurry or who don't like filling out forms. For them, simply provide multiple ways to contact you. Invite serious prospects to call to discuss their projects. When they do call, you can still use the form to gather the information you need; it's just that you will be filling it out for them.

Step 2: Qualify everyone else.

Once you've established that a new prospect fits your criteria, use the Prospect Qualifying Form (see page 210) to gather the additional information you need.

PROSPECT QUALIFYING FORM

Company:
Contact name:
Title:
Address and phone:
URL:
Assistant's name:
Industry:
Source:
Lead from:
Referral from:
Web search:
Response to promo sent:

Other:

QUALIFYING QUESTIONS TO ASK

What design firms have you used in the past?

What needs do you have throughout a typical year?

What is your role in the company?

Are you looking for strategic direction or execution of your projects?

What have you appreciated/not appreciated about the design firms you've worked with in the past?

Why are you are considering working with us?

What kind of people do you like to work with?

What is your budget?

Step 3: Make sure there's a financial fit.

There is one question you must ask and get answered in your initial contact with a new prospect before you proceed to any next steps: You must find out if they can afford you. If you fail to address this issue before agreeing to write a proposal, chances are you will waste a lot of time.

If your prospects are focused on their needs, asking you all sorts of questions about everything but money, then it's your responsibility to bring it up. It may feel strange or mercenary to address the issue of money so early in the relationship, but you need to make sure you're on the same page.

Don't assume they don't want to give you their budget. Some prospects want to give you as much information as possible so you can give them an accurate number. They don't want to waste their time, either. So don't make any assumptions, just ask all your questions. It can be as simple as asking, "What's your budget?" And sometimes they will simply tell you. Other times, you may have to be more creative.

For example, you can ask for three things, one of which is the budget. That way, the question about money is couched in and around other equally important issues and becomes part of the conversation. Say, "There are three things I need to know first: What is the project, what is your time frame and what is your budget?"

They may just come right out right and say, "All right, we will have $XX in our budget." Don't be impulsive; restrain yourself. Sometimes they will surprise you. Even if it's more than you anticipated or would ever have asked for, keep a poker face and say, "I'll get back to you."

Likewise, when they ask for a price, even if you're being pressured, don't blurt out a number. Resist the temptation to put a number on the table just to get it over with. If you do that and the client quickly says, "Okay," you know your number is too low. Take your time. And don't forget: This is a conversation.

If you're not getting anywhere, try this: "I just want to make sure we're on the same page financially, so it would help to know your budget or at least the range of what you're thinking of spending on this project."

On the other hand, while money should be part of the first conversation, it shouldn't be the focus. So if your prospect's goal in the first conversation is to get a firm price from you, especially without much conversation, consider it a red flag, but respond with a range. If they say, "How much is a web site?" your response should be something like, "Well, it can range anywhere from $5,000 to $25,000. Is that within your budget?"

If they don't have a budget or, for whatever reason, don't want to tell you what it is, that is also a good time to propose a range. You are simply throwing numbers around to determine whether it's worth continuing the conversation, for both of you. You can even use that language to address the issue: "Let's throw out some numbers to make sure we're in the same ballpark. A simple web site usually runs $5,000, while a more complex one could be as high as $25,000. How does that fit into your budget?"

If $5,000 is within their range, they'll say so. But if what they had in mind (and may not have known it) was $500, you'll be able to tell right away, and that may end the conversation right there. You just saved yourself a lot of time and energy by not pursuing a non-project.

CHARGING FOR AN INITIAL CONSULTATION

Instead of offering the first needs assessment meeting at no charge, try putting a price on it. Position it as a "consultation"—use that word—and offer to meet for a working meeting rather than a "show-and-tell" sales meeting. Tell them what they'll get and why it's better than a "getting to know you" meeting.

Here's how it might sound: "During our initial consultation, we'll give you an idea about what we would do if we were awarded this project. If you like the ideas, we'll create a proposal based on these ideas. If not, we both walk away with something. The fee for the initial consultation is $500, and it would be applied to your job if you decide to hire us for the project."

Step 4: Meet to assess their needs.

Once you've qualified your prospects and established that you can do what they need and they can afford you, the next step is to meet more formally to find out more, whether in person (which is always preferable) or on the phone. Either way, the objective of this meeting is to assess their needs before giving fixed prices.

Here's what often happens. That first meeting is going great. Everyone is getting along beautifully. They love your work. You love that they love your work. You are excited about the project and already have a ton of ideas that you're having trouble keeping to yourself (which you don't necessarily need to do, by the way—just don't give away the farm quite yet). It looks like they have money to spend. You can already see the dancing dollars.

You talk about the project specs, and the ideas, and the colors and the type—all the good stuff designers love to talk about. Then you must transition from that warm and fuzzy part of the conversation into the real money discussion.

Voice control is important here. You must be relaxed and confident. If your voice starts to flutter when you start talking about money, it tells the client you are unsure of your value.

There is no need for a big dramatic segue. Just say, "Okay, let's talk about money." That's it. Shift the conversation to budget with one simple sentence.

GETTING CLIENTS TO TALK ABOUT THEIR BUDGETS

Once you've initiated the conversation, now what? What should you say? What if there's silence? What if they say, "Okay," and wait for you to go on? Have your questions ready.

Question 1: Can you spend X, Y or Z?

You've probably had your share of prospects who say, "I just have no idea how much this kind of thing costs," and that may be true. But don't let that stop you from finding out their budget. They have a number in their minds, whether they know it or not. And that's where you use The Magic Three.

You give them three numbers: a low one, a mid-range one and a high one. Say, "Well, you must have an idea of how much you want to spend. Is it as low as $1,000, as much as $5,000, or up to $20,000?" Try using your hands to gesture low, middle and high. This visual helps to engage them in the conversation with you.

By asking this question, you're not saying, "This can be done for $1,000, $5,000 or $20,000." Your position is: "What number do you have in your mind, and I'll tell you what I can do for that number." You're asking for their parameters because you want to fall within them. If you don't know their parameters, your chances of falling within them are low.

Question 2: What did you spend on this project last time?

Your prospects may be more inclined to talk about what they spent before or what somebody else in their position spent. Alternately, you can ask, "Is this first time you're doing this project?" or "Did you do this project last year?"

Question 3: What did you plan to spend on this project?

Another approach is to put the design or marketing project in context. Go beyond the design budget and ask about the total budget. For example, if your prospect is opening a restaurant, the question would be, "How much are you spending on this restaurant?" Or for an event, "How much is this event costing you? Is this a $50,000 event? Or a $500,000 event?"

That way, you can calculate a percentage of a bigger number to determine what they may be able to afford for design.

SAVING THE DAY AND MAKING THEM PAY

Peleg shares a story of a client who came to Top Design after engaging another designer to design a poster. The first designer did an abysmal job, even after twelve rounds of revisions. The client said to Peleg, "I need you to save this project for me."

They discussed the project specs and the content, and when it was time to talk about money, Peleg said, "Okay, let's talk about money. I realize you have already spent some money on this project, so I'm curious to know what you have left in your budget, because we will have to start from scratch." The client said, "Yes, I understand, but I don't know how much we have left. What do you think it will cost?"

So Peleg used The Magic Three. He said, "Tell me where you fall on this spectrum. Is it as low as $5,000?" He started with this number because he knew he didn't want to touch this project for less than $5,000. "Is it as much as $10,000? Or up to 15,000?"

The client's response was, "Well, we can probably do $15,000." Peleg was surprised. The number he was going to suggest was $5,000, but because he waited and asked the right questions, he ended up charging $12,000, which was still below the $15,000. The client got a bargain, and Top Design made a great profit on the job. Plus, the client thinks Peleg is a hero!

So the lesson is: Don't assume anything when it comes to money. And especially don't assume they'll always go for the lowest number you offer. Cheap prices often indicate low quality, and smart clients value quality. For that reason alone, they usually won't choose your lowest number.

When They Won't or Don't Give You a Budget

You may try all of these techniques, and your prospects still resist giving you a number. What do you do?

Tell them you'll get back to them. Then take some time and come up with a figure that reflects what the project is worth to you. Then, before putting anything on paper, run the number by your prospect for a thumbs up or thumbs down.

IF THEY SAY...

If they say..."Just give me a price."

...then you say, "There's no way I can tell you how much something like this will cost without knowing more details."

If they say..."Just tell me your hourly rate."

...then you say, "We don't have an hourly rate. Tell me what you need, I'll tell you how much it costs."

If they say..."Why does my budget matter? Just tell me the costs."

...then you say, "What we produce can be almost infinitely tailored to meet a client's specific needs. So, we need to have an idea of what you think is suitable." With this response, you're telling the client, "We can do whatever you want. The question is, how much do you want to spend?" That's why that matters. Remember, you're not selling something off a menu.

Don't Talk About the Price of the Work in Your Portfolio

If you are meeting in person (or even virtually) and you are showing examples from your portfolio, don't say, "This brochure cost $5,000." It may seem like a safe strategy, but, in fact, it can be dangerous. That brochure may have cost $5,000 because it was five years ago and you did it for a dream client in two weeks with no revisions and no headaches. Every project is different; every client is different. There are too many factors involved to quote based on past projects.

If you need to talk about price as it relates to the work in your portfolio, give a range. Or say, "Something like this could cost up to $5,000."

Talking about money may never be comfortable for you, but the more practice you get, the easier it will become and the more confident you'll feel.

Now that you have qualified your prospect and you know they can afford you, you are ready to consider writing a proposal.

CHAPTER 10
WHAT SHOULD BE IN MY PROPOSAL?

Proposals—documents that detail what you propose to do for a client and under what terms—are essential to the selling process, especially if you're pursuing complex projects from large corporations. The objective of your proposal is to position you, your approach and your strategy to the prospect. It should demonstrate your expertise and look good visually. But writing proposals can be very time-consuming, so don't do it unless it's a productive use of your time. In other words, just because someone asks for a proposal doesn't mean you should always provide it.

YOUR PROPOSAL IS A MARKETING TOOL

Every communication between you and your prospect is part of your marketing effort, including your proposal.

By this point in the process, you will have had multiple communications with your prospect during which you've addressed the important issues and asked all the right questions, so the proposal essentially is a detailed confirmation or recap of what's been discussed. There shouldn't be any surprises.

Tailor a Template

Most proposals are too long and filled with too much generic material, often included to create heft rather than substance. That's one reason why prospects simply flip to the last page to find "the number" then end up comparing apples to oranges when they look at your competitors' proposals side-by-side.

You should have a template for your proposals so you don't have to reinvent the wheel each time you create one. You can hire a copywriter to draft a proposal template for you, which you can then reuse by either tweaking it or going back to the writer to revise it for a new project.

But the proposals you submit should be anything but generic. Once you've taken the time to find out as much as you can about the project, customize your proposal so that it reads like a document written expressly for this prospect. Another objective of the proposal is to demonstrate your understanding of your prospective client's project or challenge. So don't do it at 3 A.M. the night before it's due. Give yourself enough time to complete it, let it rest a day or so, then look at it again before you submit it. Here is a sample proposal from Peleg Top.

PROPOSAL FOR CREATIVE SERVICES

TOP DESIGN

Date
Client Name
Client Organization
Client Street Address

Client City, State, Zip

Project: Logo, identity and website art direction

PROJECT OBJECTIVES:

- To create a brand presence for_____
  _{CLIENT}
  and overall online brand presence

- To develop corporate identity and business communications collateral to support the web site and its launch, to work together with PR agency to implement launch.

PHASE I: DISCOVERY

Prior to beginning any program, we need to learn as much as possible about your company and product. We need to gain a clear understanding of your vision and goals. We also must define the scope and parameters of this project and define how they fit within your strategic objectives. We have refined our approach to "getting our arms around" your group to ensure that our work is built on a solid foundation.

The initial phase of our project together will include:

- A kick-off meeting

- Brand immersion discovery and research

- Developing a brand study board

- Identifying subjective preferences

- Developing a creative brief

- Reviewing and assessing site map and architecture

- Creating usability recommendations based on architecture supplied by client

- An audience audit and overview profile

- A brand characteristics overview

DELIVERABLE: creative brief and design direction report

PHASE II: VISUALIZE

Once we clearly define your goals and objectives and understand the findings of the brand study, we begin the conceptual development of the logo and identity. This is a crucial stage for developing the final logo solution as it defines the scope and direction of work to be included in the style guide.

This phase will include:

- Design development of logo and overall brand identity

- Typography treatment study

- Color treatments application

- Storyboards for look and feel for the site, interface design elements

- The design, layout and positioning of the overall styling for the site's landing page and two subsequent layers

- Up to three initial design story-board concepts presented to demonstrate styling options (from the initial presentation, up to three rounds of revisions are included in the budget)

- Feedback from client and revisions

- Refinement of branding, design and copy in all materials

DELIVERABLE: logo and brand identity, web site design direction look and feel

PHASE III: CREATE / DESIGN IMPLEMENTATION

Once design direction has been approved by _____,
CLIENT NAME
our team will proceed to produce the following items:

1. Web site design implementation: bringing the approved design to electronic files for all required pages on the web site

   - Create cascading style sheets for each of the core pages (current wireframes demonstrate eight core pages, however, additional pages will likely require unique style sheets)

   - The final deliverable is layered Photoshop files ready for programming, a base-series of html style sheets (CSS), demonstrating up to three layers of GUI (budget is based on a range of 10–20 style sheetpages)

2. Design of business communication collateral

   - business cards, stationery, second sheets, envelopes, mailing labels
   - press kit folder

DELIVERABLE: Print collateral ready to print, cascading style sheet (CSS) for main pages

BUDGET AND TIMELINES:

Phase I: Discovery	$5,000	(2–3 weeks)
Phase II: Visualize	$16,000	(6–8 weeks)
Phase III: Create	$18,000–$24,000	(4–6 weeks)
• Additional style sheets	$1,500 each	
Copywriting services	$5,000–$12,000	(4–6 weeks)
• Tagline development		
• Web site marketing copy		
Marketing plan development	$6,000–$18,000	(6–8 weeks)

TERMS:

Project schedule: Upon acceptance of our proposal, Top Design Studio will submit a preliminary schedule along with a project agreement, terms and conditions.

- Upon receiving a signed work agreement the first payment in the amount of $21,000 is due to start project.

- Additional payments are due prior to proceeding with additional phases, 50% deposit and balance COD.

** Printing costs will be determined upon approval of art direction and design.

This proposal is made on January 25th, 2007, by Peleg Top Incorporated, dba Top Design Studio for _____. When this estimate

CLIENT

is approved by_____, a work agreement will be sent

CLIENT NAME

What You Need Before You Write

Your prospects may provide "creative briefs" or some guidelines for the project they have in mind. But whether or not they do, make sure you have all the information you need before you begin writing the proposal. This may require a phone call or even an in-person meeting, depending on the size of the project. Serious prospects will agree to meet with you and may even appreciate taking the extra time early on in the project to get things right. What you find out in that meeting may not be in the creative brief prepared by your prospect and will give you an edge over your competition. In addition, you'll get a feel for the personality of your client, and you can establish a rapport that may help you land the job. Don't spend too much time chatting though—remember that your goal is to get accurate information.

GET HELP

Sometimes it will be to your benefit to hire a copywriter to help you write a large proposal, especially if the project also calls for a copywriter to be involved. Consider inviting the copywriter to the initial meeting with your prospect to gather the information needed to write the proposal and, hopefully, to do the work. The copywriter must understand the complete scope of the project and will probably ask questions you wouldn't think of. Plus, if you work independently, showing up with a colleague doubles the impression your prospect has of you and your staff, making you look bigger and perhaps more of a contender, depending on the prospect.

Negotiate with the copywriter about a fee for this upfront work. Some will agree to invest the time in exchange for the opportunity to be brought in on the project if it is awarded to you. Indeed, you're helping market their services, and there's a value associated with that. Some copywriters, however, may not have the time to invest and will require a fee. Don't hesitate to pay them to write your proposal if it will increase your own chances of getting the project.

Responding to a Request for Proposal (RFP)

If you receive an RFP that already provides a structure for your proposal, don't even think about submitting your generic proposal. Your prospect needs to compare apples to apples. Make contact with the prospect to clarify anything you don't understand about the proposal or the project. In fact, this is a good idea even if you think you understand everything. This conversation will also make you stand out from those who simply receive the RFP and submit their proposals without any actual contact.

PRE-PROPOSAL CHECKLIST

Here is a checklist of questions to ask, besides the usual time frame and budget parameters, to create a proposal that will get you the job.

What are the big-picture goals of this project?

What is the specific objective you need to achieve?

How will you measure the success of this project?

What/who is the market for this project?

Who is the main decision-maker on this project?

What models are you using for this project?

Where is the source content coming from?

How much research will be necessary?
Are there specific technologies you do or do not want used?
How does this project fit into your big picture?
Have you ever done something like this before? If so, what?

WHAT SHOULD BE IN MY PROPOSAL?

There are three types of proposals, but they all have these core elements:

- **Brief project description:** what they need and what you are proposing to do

- **Deliverables:** what they get, when, how many, etc.

- **Costs:** creative fees plus expenses, expressed as ranges rather than fixed prices to provide a cushion in case things change, as they often do

- **Timeline:** realistic production schedule

- **Sign-off:** the client's approval of agreement

Even if you're doing a short proposal, it's important to include this basic information. If you are doing a more lengthy proposal, you also can consider including:

- **Information about your firm.** This includes your biography and those of any other relevant contributors and freelancers on the project.

- **Samples.** Even if they've already visited your web site or seen samples of your work, by the time your proposal arrives (along with a few others), it will help your prospects to see relevant samples when they're making this decision. The proposal also may be reviewed by others involved in the decision-making process who are not familiar with your work.

- **References.** References communicate credibility. Strategically choose one or two client references whose projects have something in common with this new one. Then, let your references know you're passing along their names. (It's a great excuse to make contact and see if they need anything from you, too.) Tell them a bit about the prospective project, and give them some details about what your prospect may be most interested hearing about.

- **Usage rights.** Briefly clarify how and where the work will be used, per your discussions so far. You will go into more detail about this in the contract.

- **Client responsibility.** This is a list of what the clients are responsible for, which also makes it easy for them to see the level of their involvement.

Some designers submit proposals that double as contracts by adding terms and conditions. But unless it's a sure thing that you're getting the project, the first version of your proposal should not include any legal language. Simply include a phrase at the end such as, "Upon approval of this proposal, we will send a contract."

THREE TYPES OF PROPOSALS

One-page estimate. This essentially is a confirmation letter or cost estimate for small projects or projects for an ongoing client. It should take no more than fifteen minutes to create.

Small proposal (1–3 pages). The structure of this proposal is very close to that of the one-pager. It outlines the bare bones of a project but goes into more detail because it's used most often with a new prospect who doesn't know your work or your process. It shouldn't take more than an hour to create, and it can include information about your process or methodology, especially if your prospect has not worked with a design firm before.

Large proposal (20+ pages). For a major project, the large proposal is an important marketing tool. As a general rule, the more you charge, the more pages you should include in your proposal. Use it to position yourself or your firm as an expert, demonstrating that you have the experience and knowledge for the prospect's specific project. The longer document provides substance and shows that you've thought through the project all the way. It can take a day or more to create, depending on the complexity. This is the time to hire a professional copywriter because for a proposal at this level,

> the client has higher expectations and often requires more copy. On the pricing page, it's best to give one total number or range of prices instead of providing a separate fee for each deliverable or phase proposed.

Don't Forget the Cover Letter

Whether or not you present the proposal in person, always include a cover letter, another strategic marketing tool used to highlight the main features of your proposal. It's also the appropriate place for any extraneous material that doesn't belong in the proposal.

In the cover letter, begin by thanking your prospect for considering your proposal. From there, outline what was discussed about the important aspects of the project. This shows you have listened and understood. Go on to describe why you are qualified for this project. Highlight your past experience and your expertise, even if it's also included in the proposal. Remember, the prospect may not read every word.

SAMPLE PROJECT PROCESS AND TIMELINE

Here's an example of Top Design's project process and timeline for a logo and identity project. Note that it outlines the five meetings and has space to fill in the date for each one. These dates are chosen during the first meeting with all decision-makers present. This will ensure that your project stays on track and on deadline. If you don't lock in the dates at the outset, it may drag on indefinitely.

PHASE 1: DISCOVERY

Peleg Top, principal and creative director of Top Design Studio, along with the project team, will meet with you, the client, to identify preferences, discuss possible thematic approaches, collect data, background information and reference materials, clarify all needs and establish parameters. We will prepare a creative brief for you to review. Once the creative brief is approved, we will proceed to the work on the next phase.

DELIVERABLE: CREATIVE BRIEF
Meeting #1: Discovery, creative brief intake, design intake   Date:
Meeting #2: Creative brief presentation   Date:

PHASE 2: VISUALIZE

Based on the information gathered, we will research, develop and design a variety of conceptual ideas that will strategically target your audience, product and service. We will present initial sketch concepts, gather input, make revisions and finalize the logo and identity direction.

DELIVERABLE: FINAL LOGO AND IDENTITY DIRECTION
Meeting #3: Concepts presentation   Date:

HOW SHOULD I PRESENT MY PROPOSAL?

Your proposal is not a precious document that has to be perfect. Treat it as the next step in the process. One technique you can try is to submit a "draft proposal" first. This draft proposal has no numbers or figures, only exposition about the project. Make it very clear that you're submitting the draft to make sure that you've understood their needs correctly. Once you have their feedback, make the necessary changes, add the pricing and submit it as the "final proposal." This process essentially requires prospects to read everything before going directly to the bottom line.

Present Your Proposal in Person

When your proposal is ready, do one final spell-check—you don't want to be undone by unnecessary typos. Then, don't just send it off. Remember that your proposal is one part of a conversation, and you need to be present for the response.

Don't assume prospects read your proposal thoroughly just because you send it to them, especially if you haven't submitted it as a draft first. You need to walk them through the proposal.

Whenever possible, arrange to present it in person, or at the very least, on the phone. This is an important aspect of using the proposal as a closing tool. Your prospects need to understand what you have to offer and how you are different from your competitors. They are more likely to understand this from direct contact with you than from reading your document.

However, it's not always easy to get your prospects to agree to this meeting. Start early in the process to position it as necessary. At the end of your first meeting or phone call, instead of saying, "We'll get back to you with a proposal," ask for the next meeting by saying, "When can we meet to go over the proposal?" That question implies that this is your standard process.

If they say, "Just send it to me," you can respond with, "We want to make sure you understand all the different aspects of the proposal, so we prefer to present it to you in person."

Of course, you can't force them, so if meeting face-to-face isn't feasible, go to plan B: Ask to schedule a time to present it on the phone.

SPEC WORK: SHOULD I OR SHOULDN'T I?

Although doing "spec" (short for "speculative") work is very common in some industries, such as advertising, it is not in the design industry. So the simple answer is no, you should not do spec work. That is, you should not submit work for clients who offer to pay if, and only if, they like what you do. Doing spec work devalues not only your own work, but also the graphic design profession. As a professional, you do not need to prove yourself.

If you are approached about doing spec work, you can respond with, "We're too busy with paying jobs to work on spec." You may, however, be able to transform the request into an opportunity to try the "initial consultation fee" approach. Propose to present concepts for a fee. If they like the ideas, you can proceed with the project. If not, you are paid for your time, and they have some ideas with which to work.

HOW TO ASK FOR THE SALE

Once you submit your proposal, there is more marketing to be done, more nurturing of the relationship, more showing what a pleasant and productive experience it would be to work with you. Don't just sit back and wait. Be assertive. Let your prospects know you're available to answer any questions they have. When you're marketing big-ticket creative services, your prospects may be interested, but they probably also have questions that need answers. Acknowledge their concerns and questions. Listen closely and repeat the questions back, answer them if you can or let the prospects know you'll get answers to them promptly.

Responding to "Objections"

There are a few statements that prospects use when they want to stall or aren't convinced you're the one for them. You won't always be able to work past this stage in the process, but if you back off without responding, you'll miss out on those opportunities that you can win, without knowing which ones they are. Be ready with a few ways to respond to these common "objections."

"We can't afford these prices."

Despite all your efforts to qualify your prospects upfront, you may still hear this from them. If money really is the issue, get into the specifics with them. Try breaking down the project into phases, each of which has a separate and lower price attached. This is sometimes perceived as less expensive, even though it's not. It's actually more like an a la carte menu for them to choose from. Another strategy is to revise your proposal such that it lowers the price. But avoid the temptation simply to lower your price without taking something away from what you're offering.

"We don't have the budget."

This is different from "We can't afford it." Ask what they mean by "no budget." No budget at all for this type of work? No budget left for this year? (If it's the latter, find out when the new budget starts or when budget planning will resume so you can get back in touch at that time.)

"We're staying with our current vendor."

Prospects may stay with their current resource because it's too much effort to start from scratch with someone else. Your job is to reinforce all the reasons why working with you would make their lives easier and be worth the effort to change. It may not happen this time around, but it's worth staying on their radar if you know they're itching to change.

Closing the Sale

Many designers sail through the proposal process only to lose a project because they don't know how to "close" a sale. Often, the only step missing is the last one: asking for the sale.

Try these strategies for closing the sale:

- **Outline the next step.** Say, "Have I answered all your questions? If so, and you're ready to make a decision, here's the next step in the process." Don't ever leave any doubt as to whether they have made the commitment. Ask them directly, "Are you ready to sign the contract?" or "Are you ready to schedule the first working meeting?"

- **Make it easy.** Do everything you can to make it easy for your prospects to take that next step. There should be an activity they do to make the leap from prospect to client, such as sign a contract, fill out a questionnaire or pay an invoice—something to make the process official. This also helps engender trust and professionalism. Offer to send this document rather than waiting for them to ask for it.

- **Give a deadline.** People often need to be nudged before they take action, so it's up to you to create a sense of urgency. Put a deadline on the sales process, such as "This proposal is good until the end of this month" or "We have one slot left for this month, and I'd be happy to hold it for you if you decide by Friday." The sense of urgency could tip the scales in your direction. If not, it tells you there may be something holding up the process, and you need to find out what it is. You may have a bit more selling to do.

- **Offer an incentive.** If you're sure all of your prospects' questions are answered, but they're still hesitating, try an incentive. People are so brainwashed by our consumer society that they sometimes don't buy unless they get something free. Don't resist this; go along with it. Offer a discount with a deadline, or a little something extra if they sign on before a specific date.

Finally, one caveat (and a couple of clichés): Don't count your chickens before they're hatched. Manage your expectations, and know that the deal is not sealed until the contract is signed and money has changed hands.

THREE TECHNIQUES FOR DEALING WITH THE BLACK-HOLE SYNDROME

Before you submit a proposal, you are in an ongoing dialogue with your prospects, e-mailing back and forth, confirming details via instant message. Then, as soon as you submit the proposal, silence reigns, and you never hear from them again.

People are so busy that they rarely take the time to let you know what happened with a project you didn't get. It's not courteous, and it's not professional, but it's becoming the norm. There may have been a shift in priorities, or they awarded the project to someone else. You may never find out what happened, and sometimes you have to accept that fact.

However, don't disappear into that black hole yourself. Stay in the game. Here are three ways to do just that:

1. **Leave a final message.** If it's clear that the project is not going to happen in the way and within the time frame you'd anticipated, don't just slink away. Put some closure to the process by leaving a final voice mail message along these lines: "I haven't heard from you, so I don't know what happened with the proposal we sent, but it looks like it's not going to happen within the time frame we discussed. So

I just wanted to let you know that we're still interested in pursuing this if and when you are. I will touch base again in a month." Then send that same message via e-mail, so they have it in writing (and because they just may respond to this).

2. **Check in to see how it's going.** This is especially important if they did award the project to someone else. Let some time go by, then call to see how it's going. They may have chosen the low bidder and are paying for it now with low-quality work. If you happen to call and things aren't going well, you might be just the solution to their problems.

3. **Stay in touch.** Obviously, you shouldn't stalk your prospects, but you also mustn't drop out of sight. Let your marketing kick in by staying in touch via your e-mail newsletter or other ongoing tools.

What to Do if You Don't Get the Project

You had high hopes. They seemed enthusiastic, but when you get the call (or more likely the e-mail message), you find out you weren't chosen. It's hard not to be disappointed. But the reality is that this is part of doing business. If you get one out of every two proposals, you're doing well.

That's why, throughout the proposal process, it's important that you don't lose sight of the big picture. Don't assume this project is the one and only opportunity you'll have to work with this prospect. Think about this as your first proposal, the beginning of a relationship. If this one doesn't materialize, know that you have had the opportunity to interact with a prospect you're interested in. The prospect has had a chance to see your work, to focus attention on it and to get to know you a bit. That's a big investment on the prospect's part. Don't drop the ball here.

Follow up graciously. Thank them for the opportunity, and lay the groundwork for the future. Let them know you'll stay in touch and would welcome another chance to submit a proposal.

Find out what they decided. Don't make any assumptions about why you didn't get the job. They may have chosen someone else, but they also may have decided not to go ahead with the project at all. There are myriad reasons why they make one choice and not another, sometimes unrelated to quality of the work or personalities of the people. Because you put so much time and energy into the proposal process, you have the right to ask for feedback. Don't ask why they didn't choose you; ask instead what choice they made and why. What was it about the designer or firm they selected that tipped the scales in their favor? They may not tell you the whole truth, but whatever feedback they give you likely will be useful for future.

Learn what you can from the experience, whether it's related to the proposal process, to that prospect specifically or to the industry in general. Take the learning one step further and outline in writing how and what you will do differently next time. This helps to solidify the lessons.

And don't put too much weight on the proposal, because there is more to the selling process than what's on paper. What matters more is how well you communicate, how reliable you are, how you speak to them and how well taken care of they feel, including through the follow-up process.

CHAPTER 11
WHAT SHOULD BE IN MY CONTRACT?

Note: This chapter refers to legal aspects of doing business, and because we're not lawyers, we won't go into detail about those legal aspects. However, we have interviewed lawyers for their perspectives and will point to resources where actual legal advice can be found.

NEGOTIATING THE CONTRACT

You've submitted your proposal, you've answered your prospects' questions about it, you've waited for them to make a decision and finally, the call comes: You got the job!

It's not time to celebrate just yet. Before you get to work on the project, there is some business to take care of. Don't skip past this all-important step just because you or your clients are eager to get started on the fun part. Never ever start the project until you have successfully negotiated (and signed) the contract and have a deposit in hand.

You may worry that a contract will scare off your clients, maybe even that they will choose a different designer who doesn't make them sign a contract. But if your prospects are bona fide professionals, signing a contract won't be a problem. They will respect you all the more for having one. If they do resist, take it as one more red flag and beware.

Your business may feel like a very friendly enterprise and you may enjoy your clients, but don't be mistaken. Anything can happen. People change their minds. Priorities get reconfigured, budgets are discontinued, companies are bought and sold. New bosses make unanticipated changes. Things are bound to go wrong, and you need to be protected. Your rights can be abused out of sheer ignorance rather than any malicious intent, simply because you don't have the proper systems in place—including a contract to protect you and your work.

What Is a Contract, and Why Do I Need One?

A contract is a document that outlines the terms and conditions under which you will perform your work. It clearly states the responsibilities of both parties and what will happen should problems arise.

The most obvious reason for a contract is to protect yourself and your company. When you sell your work, you essentially are selling a right to your property—in this case, your intellectual property, which is intangible. And because it's intangible, the process may be less clear than if the object in question were a tangible object, like a car or a house.

According to Olivera Medenica, partner at Wahab & Medenica LLC, a law firm in New York City that specializes in intellectual property, when you create an illustration, the actual illustration is not the extent of your property. You have more than that to sell. You have a bundle of rights, including a property right in the actual illustration and in any derivative work, such as other ways the illustration can be used. You must determine how much of that bundle of rights you will sell and how much you will keep. Are you selling a license to use the design for a limited time or purpose? Will you retain the right to reuse the illustration or a version of it for another project? Will you retain the right to use it in your portfolio? On your web site? Or are you selling it outright, as in a "work for hire" agreement? All of these things need to be spelled out.

As for whether you should do work for hire, the Graphic Artists Guild advises against it. In reality, the bigger your client, the less ownership you are likely to retain of the work you create. Plus, design isn't considered to be "art" the way illustration and photography are. If you decide to do work for hire, the best strategy is this: The fewer rights you retain, the higher your upfront fee should be.

Ideally, you only will need to negotiate once at the beginning of each relationship. Then all future projects can refer back to the terms that are already in place, using a simple agreement (the one-pager) for each additional project contracted.

Beyond providing legal protection, a contract plays a role in your positioning. When you send a contract to a client, you convey this important message: "I am a professional, and I take this work seriously." This puts you in a position of strength and shows your client that you understand the value of your work. And taking your business seriously demonstrates that you will take the client's business seriously.

What Can a Contract Protect a Designer From?

A contract does not guarantee that someone will not abuse the rights to your work, but it puts you at an advantage if someone does abuse your rights. Without a contract, you have very little grounds for a lawsuit. Olivera says, "Attorneys are not magicians. They need proof. A contract provides that proof, and it will help you get an attorney to take your case on contingency. That means you don't have to pay legal fees and the attorney only recovers damages once you recover them. With a contract, everything is spelled out as to who owns what. Without a contract, it's 'he said, she said.'"

Olivera also strongly recommends registering all work (except work done for hire) with the federal government's copyright office. "It's cheap and makes a huge difference," she says, "and will help in a lawsuit." That doesn't mean you have to register every single design separately. You can register a series of designs. (It's all explained at www.copyright.gov.)

Have Your Own Contract

It's important that you present your own contract instead of signing one initiated by your clients because theirs is written with their interests in mind, not yours. When you respond to "You got the job" with "Great, I'll send you my contract," it shows you're setting the rules. They will have an opportunity to modify your contract, but at least the starting point issues from your perspective.

TURNING YOUR PROPOSAL INTO A CONTRACT

Because there is some overlapping information between a proposal (especially a large proposal) and a contract—such as payment terms, schedule and deadlines, and usage rights—it is relatively easy to modify a proposal into a contract. You may simply take out the self-promotional elements (such as portfolio samples and bios), elaborate on whatever needs more detail for the contract version and add the appropriate terms and conditions. You'll have a complete document to use as the starting point for your negotiations with the client. When signed by both parties, the complete document will be your contract.

Instead of distributing the contract as a PDF document, consider distributing it as a Word document so that the client can make (and track) changes to the text. This will save you a lot of time and speed up the process of getting your contract signed.

The Nuts and Bolts of How to Create a Contract

Hire a lawyer to create a contract template tailored to your business that you can customize for each situation. If that's beyond your means, there are plenty of resources available, including some though the Graphic Artists Guild web site (www.gag.org).

To see another sample contract—"Standard Form of Agreement for Graphic Design Services," a free, downloadable contract from the American Institute of Graphic Arts (AIGA)—go to http://www.aiga.org/content.cfm/standard-agreement.

Once you have it in place, make sure you understand your standard contract and can speak about the various clauses and assess which ones may or may not apply to each project or client.

What Every Contract Should Have

- **Schedule:** more detailed delivery dates and scheduling than you provided in the proposal. This schedule should include target dates for clients to submit their content and for you to show concepts, comps, finished art and printing.

- **Payment terms:** when and how much you'll be paid, plus your policies regarding late charges. Outline your terms clearly. Clients with whom you've maintained long relationships should pay "net thirty," meaning they have the standard thirty days to pay. For smaller projects and for new clients, request 50 percent upfront and the balance on delivery. Being able to offer credit card payment helps because small projects can require a very quick turnaround. For large projects, consider requiring "progress payments," which are payments that are not tied directly to project milestones, but instead are tied to the calendar. For example, for a four-month project, propose four equal monthly payments (less the deposit). This way, if the project takes longer or the client has a bottleneck, your cash flow isn't affected.

- **Termination policy or cancellation clause:** as an example, "In the event of the cancellation of this assignment, a cancellation fee will be paid by the client and will include full payment for all work completed, expenses incurred and hours expended. The cancellation fee will be based on the prices outlined in the estimate/proposal. Any initial payments that have been received will be credited against any amounts due."

- **Extras:** whatever is not included in the fees, such as expenses, travel and anything else that might arise.

- **Copyright and licensing:** who owns what, usage rights and your right to compensation if the client breeches copyright. You also need copyright clearances for photographs and other additional copyrighted material. Be sure to mention in the contract whether you plan to use the work for your own marketing purposes.

- **Liability:** what happens if the project isn't completed or successful, in which case, "success" must be defined. This will minimize your liability if a campaign is unsuccessful or pulled for censorship or some other reason.

- **Errors and omissions:** who is responsible, for example, if a typo isn't caught before a piece goes to print, and what would happen in that situation.

Everything is Negotiable

Whether you are aware of it or not, you negotiate on a regular basis, not only with clients, but also with your spouse, your kids, your employees, your vendors, even with strangers getting into and out of a store or on and off a train.

A successful negotiation is a win-win, one in which both parties get at least some of what they want. Nobody gets everything they want. Compromise is at the heart of negotiation, so in order for it to be a success, start the process by keeping both parties in mind.

Once you and your client have agreed on the numbers in your proposal, turn your attention to the terms and conditions, all of which are negotiable. Your client may ask you to remove or revise one or more of your terms. You can agree to do so in exchange for something else. For example, high-profile clients may be sensitive about having their names used in your marketing. If it's important to you, you may be able to negotiate for using their names in a brochure but not showing their work on your web site, or vice versa.

Address Scope Creep Early On

When a project is not well-defined, well-planned or well-managed, or when there is a change in direction, "scope creep" sets in, which is a term for when uncontrolled changes affect the pricing. If this happens early in a project, it may be a sign that you didn't ask enough questions at the outset, or that you underestimated the project.

When this happens, above all, don't procrastinate. The most important aspect of managing scope creep is communication. As soon as you see that a project is veering off course and that you will be spending more time or more money, you must advise your client and decide together how to handle it.

If, for example, in a status meeting or phone call, it becomes obvious that what you are being asked to do is outside the scope of the project, say so right away: "That is outside the scope of the project as we outlined it in the proposal, so we'll need to review that and possibly revise the pricing. Are you aware of that?" Then, initiate a "change order" to document the changes.

It's a good idea to include a reference to scope creep in your contract so it's not a surprise. A simple paragraph that outlines the process if scope creep starts to happen will plant the necessary seed so that you can bring it up much more easily later.

Remember that a negotiation is a conversation, and the contract is the result of that conversation. Nothing is set in stone until you sign on the dotted line. Both you and your client should feel comfortable with the contract and should be able to move forward to do business.

POTENTIALLY STICKY ISSUES

WHO OWNS THE FILES?

More often than not, clients don't realize they are not buying all rights to the work you create. It's your responsibility to educate them at the beginning of the process and to ask the right questions when you set the terms. Also, don't assume they won't need the final files. Simply ask, "Do you just want the design, or do you need the files?" If they need the files, the fee you charge should be higher. Although there is no industry standard for how much to charge to hand over the art, many designers charge 50 percent of the original price. This, too, should be negotiated.

EXTRA CHORES

After you deliver a project, you may be asked to do extra chores. These may be tasks such as sending artwork to third party vendors, resizing artwork for additional use, updating the work for international use, etc. It's not easy to predict what these chores will be in advance as they often come up only after a project is complete. Don't confuse these chores with a favor your client asks of you, which takes five minutes. Your client has no idea how quickly the little chores add up—but you do. And you should be paid for them. Address the issue in advance so it isn't a surprise or an interruption to the work process. Say, "I would love to do this for you, but it doesn't fall under the scope of the project. There's a cost associated in getting all these tasks done. And that cost will be $100." If this becomes a common request with a client, propose a "miscellaneous billing" category that you can track and bill regularly.

GETTING MONEY UPFRONT
(AND WHAT CAN HAPPEN IF YOU DON'T)

No matter how you approach your payment terms—whether you require payment in three parts, two parts or monthly progress payments—you should always require a deposit to start the work.

If a client is hesitant about a deposit, consider it a red flag and be especially clear about your payment terms. You can negotiate the details of the deposit—being able to take a credit card comes in handy here, too—but don't forgo the deposit. If you do, you have no leverage if something changes or goes wrong during the project. There is no shortage of horror stories about situations that were initially friendly then turned disagreeable. Don't learn the hard way.

According to Emily Ruth Cohen, a consultant to design firms, "This simple request can often become a time-consuming struggle. Clients may give you various objections, ranging from the reasonable 'Our corporate procedures preclude me from processing any upfront payment without either receipt of work or an approved, internal purchase order' to the plausible 'As a small business, our cash flow is tight and overhead payments, like rent and utilities, may need to take priority' to the red flag 'Why should I pay for work I haven't seen yet?' or 'We don't have any money right now, but are expecting a large check soon.' Respond to these scenarios calmly and creatively.

"Emphasize that upfront payment is a reasonable request and a common procedure within the design industry. If you don't receive an upfront payment, then you are, in effect, incurring billable hours and extending credit to the client. This reasoning also can apply to asking for a deposit or retainer against out-of-pocket expenses."

MAKING IT EASY TO BE PAID BY CORPORATIONS

BY EMILY RUTH COHEN

Familiarize yourself with your client's payment policy, and keep your invoices in manageable increments. Many corporations and businesses won't pay unless an approved purchase order (P.O.) has been processed; the absence of a P.O. at the time of invoicing will delay payment.

For large expenditures, your client may have to go through several rounds of time-consuming approvals—often involving upper management and accounts payable—before a P.O. will be issued or an invoice processed. Smaller invoices often are easier to process. Ask your client how much is too much before an invoice or P.O. gets delayed because of internal processing and approval procedures. Once you know the cutoff amount for a large expenditure, you can adjust your progress payments accordingly.

When you do receive a P.O., read it carefully. Clients often will include special—often "standard"—conditions or descriptions that may or may not be appropriate or applicable to your project and relationship.

Typically, a client will compensate you for only up to 10 percent over the amount indicated in the P.O. Check with your client for the exact percentage they can or will pay. If the scope of the project changes and additional fees are incurred that exceed 10 percent of the P.O., inform the client and request a revised or additional P.O.

Many clients have an established policy for how soon they pay invoices and have timetables that range from thirty to ninety days.

It's important to find this out in advance and invoice accordingly. For example, if a client agrees to pay all invoices in "net sixty," and the project can be completed within two to three weeks, you may want to issue all invoices at the start of the project. This will help shorten the approval and processing time, and ensure that payments are made closer to the project's completion, rather than three months later. If this isn't possible, you can ask for a large percentage of your total costs to be paid upfront, thereby reducing some of your financial liability later in the project.

What to Do When Clients Don't Pay

It happens to the best of us. You've done all the right things, and clients still aren't paying up. Although you may dread dealing with this, you must. The most effective strategy is to be the squeaky wheel. That doesn't mean you should harass your clients, especially if you want to retain the working relationships. But you also can't let them take advantage of you. Simply let them know it's unacceptable not to pay according to the terms you agreed to, and that you'll stay in close touch until you are paid.

Then call every day. You may leave a lot of voice mail messages, but don't let that discourage you. You must convey the message that you won't relent. More often than not, they'll pay you just to be rid of you. Then you can decide if you want them as future clients.

Now you're on your way. You have the tools you need to get the clients you want and to run a healthy business. You're more serious about your business, and you're practicing good communication skills. And while you may not be winning every project, you are learning from every experience and you have control over your business in a way you never have before.

The challenge will be to stay in the driver's seat and build on your success. That means you must stick to your marketing schedule, or feast or famine will set in before you know it. That also means you must address conflicts or problems as soon as they arise, rather than put off what you imagine to be "difficult conversations."

Soon, you may even be thinking about taking your business to the next level.

CHAPTER 12
HOW SHOULD I GROW MY BUSINESS?

Your business is going well. You have a lot of work, and most of it is the kind of work you enjoy doing for people you like. So you think it may be time to grow your business.

But what does it mean to "grow" your business?

Everybody has a different definition. To some, growing the business means moving it out of the spare bedroom and into an office, creating an empire of sorts, hiring employees. For others, it means doing whatever it takes to make more money. Sometimes it means more overhead and more headaches, but not necessarily more money. You must decide what "growth" looks like for yourself before taking any steps.

To do that, take a good look at your business, ideally with the help of someone you trust, such as a colleague or a mentor, someone who understands your business and who is objective about it. Look at what you do well, what you find the most satisfying and which are the most lucrative clients and projects. You may be surprised at what you find. Look also at what doesn't work, where you are losing money and which clients and projects are not lucrative. That's the work you must say goodbye to and turn away when it comes again. This takes confidence at first, but as long as you have a strong marketing plan in place, you can be sure to have prospects—the good ones—in your pipeline.

You also must recognize that the only thing keeping you from getting the good clients is the time you're spending (or wasting) on your bad clients. Once you see that clearly, it becomes much easier to turn them away graciously.

THE NEXT STEPS AND WHEN TO TAKE THEM

Hiring a Tax Professional

From the very beginning, you should have a tax professional overseeing your financial process. There are many changing laws that will affect you as a business owner, and you can't spend your valuable time on that. Leave it in the hands of a professional from day one.

Incorporating Your Business

Most designers start out as sole proprietors, in which case they own everything, are personally responsible for everything that happens in the business and pay taxes as a self-employed person. If you are the only employee and you intend to keep in that way, incorporation may not be necessary.

On the other hand, incorporating or forming a limited liability company (LLC) provides what is known as the "corporate veil"—liability protection for your personal assets. This will protect you in case there is a typo on a huge print job, for example, or if clients are injured while on your premises. Other classic incorporation triggers include entering into contracts and hiring employees.

Incorporating also may offer some tax advantages to you. But either way, these decisions should be made with the help of a business attorney, as well as your accountant, because the various options have different tax implications.

Moving Out of the Spare Bedroom

It's a big leap to go from very little overhead by working from home to much more overhead by taking on the responsibility of an office space. Here are some questions to ask yourself as you consider moving your business out of your home:

- Has the size and scope of your business changed such that you no longer meet zoning regulations for home-based businesses? This might mean having customers, employees or more customers or employees than is allowed in your area.

- Is it awkward to invite clients into your home because your kids' toys are everywhere? Is your home office preventing you from pursuing larger clients because it's too far out of town to meet there?

- Is your business taking over more and more of the house and infringing on other members of the household?

- Do you have trouble staying focused or motivated in your home office? Are you easily distracted by the laundry or the refrigerator or the television?

- Are you lonely at home? Isolation is a major factor for many people to move out of the house.

If you're not quite ready for your own office space, look into executive suites that may be available in your area. They offer a good transitional step from home to traditional offices. They feature offices of varying sizes, phone and Internet service, meeting rooms and receptionists. It's an arrangement that can help you manage costs while gaining most of the benefits of a stand-alone office.

Avoiding Overwork

It's surprisingly easy to work too much when you run your own business because there is certainly always something that needs to be done. There always will be. With so much virtual working, BlackBerries, laptops and other technology that allows us to work from anywhere, it's easy to do. But you mustn't. It's essential that you know when and where and how to draw the line for yourself because business has a sneaky way of taking over your life if you allow it to. This requires discipline. Be disciplined about your time and your space.

Here are a few tips to try:

- **Create a separate physical space for your work.** And be able to close the door. That allows others to give you the privacy you need to work as well as closing the door behind you when you are finished working.

- **Create a work schedule.** Make conscious decisions about when you're working and when you're not. Then stick to those decisions. If you need one day a week with no work, make sure you take it consistently. You can make an exception on occasion, but do it deliberately, then get back on your regular schedule.

- **Organize and track your time.** One of the biggest challenges is organizing your time, especially when you're busy with client work. It's essential to prioritize what needs to be done every day with some kind of list system, either online or on a good, old-fashioned piece of paper. There will inevitably be crises that arise to interrupt your well-laid plans. But if you have your plan written down, you can turn right back to it once the fire is out. Also, tracking your time with software or simple time sheets also will allow you to see where your time is going and make some changes so that you direct the use of your time rather than letting it slip away.

- **Learn to say no.** You may be in the habit of taking whatever work comes along just because it's paying work. Or you may be a people-pleaser who doesn't like to say no. But that's not a profitable business strategy because you will end up taking on jobs that you know in your gut are a problem, and you're likely to spend too much time and aggravation getting them done. It's best to say no at the beginning and free yourself for other things.

- **Communicate your boundaries to your clients.** Make it clear at the beginning of any new business relationship what your working hours are and how and when it's best to contact you. You can have a policy whereby you don't take calls on the weekend or after hours; if you make an exception, make it clear that it's an exception. You must train your clients to work in the way you do, not the other way around. And don't always answer the phone just because it rings. If you have Caller ID and you're in the middle of a project and a client calls, you don't have to pick up.

- **Keep your business in perspective.** Business is business, nothing more. It's not your life. It's not your identity. It's not the most important thing in the world. You must be able to walk away from the work each day and not let it infiltrate the rest of your life. People who go through traumatic experiences realize quickly how unimportant business is, but you don't have to experience trauma in order to get and keep that perspective.

WHEN SHOULD I HIRE EMPLOYEES?

You may have arrived at a point where, in order to grow and get a better handle on clients and projects, you have to bring more people into your company. That means putting on the management hat. But most people are not trained to manage others, and it doesn't always come naturally.

If you want to grow your business and you think you might enjoy the challenge of managing others, start by getting some training instead of jumping into it blindly. Get a mentor, take a course and learn slowly so you feel comfortable taking each next step.

Can you derive creative satisfaction from building a business? You may not know yet. But once you start doing it, you might discover that you enjoy it, that the challenges of business development, managing money and managing people is more interesting than the creative work, which can be repetitious and boring.

It's best to hire employees who can do what you can't, or who are better than you at the things you don't like to do. So if you need help with the creative work, collaborate with somebody who can complement your talents. If you don't like the administrative aspects of business, hire a good administrative assistant who can keep your office organized. It may even be possible to find someone who has both of those skills. Look for a design student who understands that design is, after all, a business.

SHOULD MY ASSISTANTS WORK ON-SITE?

Do you have space for them? Should you make space for them? Many people telecommute or work virtually these days. There are tools that facilitate the process, so it's a good way to start out. But if you miss the personal interaction that comes with having someone in your office, start with a student who can work for a semester or two.

Use a revenue target—an amount of money you are bringing in regularly over the course of a year—to determine when to add to your overhead. That number will be determined by a variety of factors, but it will probably be more than $100,000.

You also need to have money in the bank to get through your first year or two. Aim to have two to four months of overhead sitting in a money market account earning interest. Don't touch that money unless you absolutely must. If you do, it means there's something wrong, and it needs to be fixed.

Don't go into debt or start charging business expenses to your credit card in order to grow your business. Depending on where you live, there may be economic development grants or low-cost loans available to support your growth.

For most people, though, taking that next step is a leap of faith. Can you look at your clients and the projects on your plate and say, "These people are going to be around next month and the month after that, so I can take the risk"? Because it is a risk, and you need to be ready for it.

STEPS YOU CAN TAKE TOWARD GROWTH

1. **Make the transition while employed.** When you launch full-time, you'll need a cushion to live off of for six months to a year. So the ideal situation may be to start you own businesses while you have a job—you can work on your business after hours and on weekends. That allows you to save some money to invest in your business while you also research the market you want to focus on and start making connections.

2. **Start by hiring freelancers.** Hiring freelancers to work with you on a contract basis will give you a taste of giving direction, supervising the work and making sure your standards are enforced. Or hire a student or intern for a month or two. This can be a good way to find out what it's like to be responsible for another person before you take on someone else's paycheck.

3. **Learn to delegate.** Delegating is letting go. As a boss, your job is to get out of your employees' way and make sure they have the environment and the tools they need to do a great job. From there, it's all about communication. Check in on a regular basis or at certain points in the project for a progress report.

And, of course, remember to keep marketing your services to grow your business. Otherwise, you know what happens: that pesky feast-or-famine syndrome. In slow periods, use your time, money and creativity to get your name out there. Make a few phone calls, ramp up the networking. There's always something you can do to bring in more work. It's just a question of sitting down and doing it rather than waiting for the work to walk in the door.

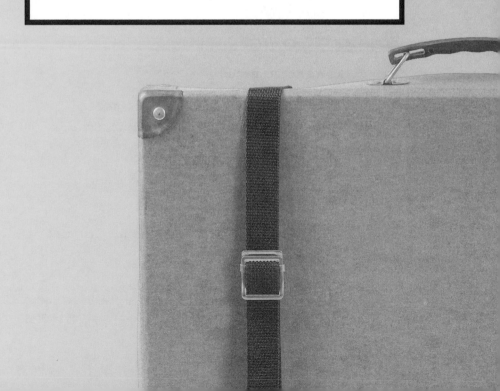

RESOURCES

Below are lists of recommended books, links and magazines.

BOOKS

By Ilise Benun

Stop Pushing Me Around!: A Workplace Guide for the Timid, Shy, and Less Assertive

The Art of Self Promotion

PR for Dummies (Second Edition)

Designing Websites:// for Every Audience

Self-Promotion Online: Marketing Your Creative Services Using Web Sites, E-Mail and Digital Portfolios

By Peleg Top, Top Design

Design for Special Events: 500 of the Best Logos, Invitations and Graphics

Letterhead & Logo Design 8

Other Books We Recommend:

The Business Side of Creativity: The Complete Guide for Running a Graphic Design or Communications Business by Cameron S. Foote

The Graphic Designer's Guide to Pricing, Estimating & Budgeting by Theo Stephan Williams

The Savvy Designer's Guide to Success: Ideas and Tactics for a Killer Career by Jeff Fisher

Talent Is Not Enough: Business Secrets for Designers
by Shel Perkins

WEB SITES AND BLOGS

www.marketing-mentor.com

Home of Marketing Mentor, the coaching program for creatives founded by Ilise Benun and Peleg Top

www.artofselfpromotion.com

Archive of resources and articles published in print form by Ilise Benun

www.marketingmixblog.com

The official blog of Marketing Mentor and the community that's sprung up around it

www.creativebusiness.com

Cameron Foote's site, chock full of resources, forms, articles and much more

www.recourses.com

David Baker's site with useful position papers and articles, plus info about his consulting services

www.emilycohen.com

Emily Cohen's site has excellent resources from this consultant to creatives

www.smallbusinessadvocate.com

Jim Blasingame's overwhelmingly resourceful site for small business owners

www.askjim.biz

A "get-your-questions-answered" site for small business owners

www.marketingprofs.com

Resource site that provides marketing know-how through newsletters, online seminars and more

http://businessofdesignonline.com

Blog by designers that focuses on, yes, the business of design

www.creativelatitude.com

A worldwide community that unites various creative disciplines for collective promotion, education and ethical business practice

http://blog.sessions.edu

Curated blog from the online school, Sessions Online School of Design

http://biznik.com

A business-building social network for indie professionals

www.linkedin.com

Online business network of millions of professionals around the world in 150 industries

www.functionfox.com

Provides simple, secure, web-based time-tracking and billing tools

www.myemma.com

Easy to use, designer-friendly e-mail marketing distribution system

MAGAZINES

HOW

Print

STEP Inside Design

Dynamic Graphics

INDEX

MARKETING MENTOR FREE ADVICE!

This is where we practice what we preach. We want to learn about you so we can provide information and services to help you build your business. In return, we offer you a free, half-hour phone consultation, during which we will answer your three most pressing marketing questions and, if you're interested, tell you how the Marketing Mentor coaching programs can help your business grow. Just fill out this form and fax it back to 866-854-5810. We'll e-mail you to schedule the free phone consultation.

Ilise Benun | www.marketing-mentor.com

Name:	Company name:

City, State and Country:

Phone number and time zone:

E-mail address:

Web address:

Best time to talk:

CHECK ALL THAT APPLY

What is your biggest obstacle to marketing?
- ☐ I have no time to do it.
- ☐ It's too overwhelming.
- ☐ It's too expensive.
- ☐ I don't like it.

What do you need to learn?
- ☐ How to develop the self-confidence I need to get the word out.
- ☐ How to set realistic marketing goals and a plan to achieve them.
- ☐ How to feel comfortable networking with anyone.
- ☐ How to ask for what I need: money, information, projects, contacts, etc.

What would you like to accomplish?
- ☐ Develop a cold calling campaign to a specific market.
- ☐ Develop a new web site (or revamp an old one).
- ☐ Drive traffic to my web site.
- ☐ Develop an email marketing campaign.
- ☐ Other:_____
  _____

What kind of help do you need?
- ☐ A partner to bounce ideas off of.
- ☐ A professional to guide me.
- ☐ A catalyst to inspire me to achieve my goals.
- ☐ Someone to keep my marketing on track.